A Promise
TO
Ourselves

Alec Baldwin
with Mark Tabb

A Promise
TO
Ourselves

*A Journey Through
Fatherhood and Divorce*

ST. MARTIN'S PRESS ⚏ NEW YORK

This book is sold with the understanding that neither the publisher nor the author is engaged in rendering legal or other professional services. If legal advice or other expert assistance is required, the services of a competent professional should be sought.

www.stmartins.com

Design by Elina D. Nudelman

Library of Congress Cataloging-in-Publication Data

Baldwin, Alec, 1958–
    A promise to ourselves: a journey through fatherhood and divorce / Alec Baldwin.—1st ed.
      p. cm.
    ISBN-13: 978-0-312-36336-9
    ISBN-10: 0-312-36336-2
    1. Baldwin, Alec, 1958—Divorce. 2. Actors—United States—Biography. 3. Custody of children—United States—Case studies.
4. Divorced fathers—Legal status, laws, etc.—United States. I. Title.
    PN2287.B157A3 2008
    792.02'8092—dc22
    [B]   2008016510

First Edition: September 2008

10 9 8 7 6 5 4 3 2 1

To Ireland, for showing

To Nicole, for caring

To Beth, for listening

And to my mother, Carol Baldwin, for ringing

Contents

The Lamb

Little Lamb, who made thee?
Does thou know who made thee?
Gave thee life & bid thee feed
By the stream & o'er the mead;
Gave thee clothing of delight,
Softest clothing woolly bright;
Gave thee such a tender voice,
Making all the vales rejoice?
Little Lamb who made thee?
Does thou know who made thee?

Little Lamb, I'll tell thee,
Little Lamb, I'll tell thee:
He is called by thy name,
For he calls himself a Lamb.
He is meek, & he is mild;
He became a little child.
I a child, & thou a lamb,
We are called by His name,
Little Lamb, God bless thee!
Little Lamb, God bless thee!

—*William Blake*

A common way in which a parent will contribute to the alienation is to view as "harassment" the attempts on the part of the hated parent to make contact with the children. The alienated parent expresses interest by telephone calls, attempts at visitation, the sending of presents, etc. These are termed "harassment" and the children themselves come to view such overtures similarly. In frustration the parent increases efforts in these areas, thereby increasing the likelihood that the attempts will be viewed as nuisances.

—Richard A. Gardner, M.D.

"Recent Trends in Divorce and Custody Litigation,"
Academy Forum, vol. 29, no. 2,
1985, pp. 3–7

A Promise
TO
Ourselves

Introduction

I NEVER WANTED TO write this book. Although my experiences with judges, lawyers, and court-ordered therapists during my own high-conflict divorce proceedings left me outraged over the injustices I believe are endemic to the family law system in our society, I had no desire to revisit them. The pain I suffered, the fear of and anger I felt toward nearly all of the principals involved, and the inescapable sense of helplessness and isolation exhausted me. However, to live inside the divorce matrix, to be engaged in that battle, ultimately means to be poised to tell your story, to make your point, to argue your side at a moment's notice. It is a fire that is constantly burning.

These feelings moved me to share my own experiences with nearly any kindred spirit who broached the subject. In restaurants, ticket lines, airplanes, men's locker rooms, wherever I might be, when that particular conversation started, the facts of my own case would spill out in a torrent.

Other times I would sit and listen for hours, grateful for the opportunity to allow someone else to unburden themselves. I could never tell my story urgently enough, and I never tired of the subject of divorce's iniquities. I believed that a book on the subject would write itself.

Eventually, that would change. The passion I had for this issue dried up. The ideas and stories, once so fresh in my mind that I thought they would pour out of me and onto the page like a Pollock painting, began to fade. For three years I had told my story, each recitation as fresh as the first. But any normal human being has a limited capacity for ongoing conflict, and I believed I had reached mine. I have heard people use terms like *spent* and *hollowed out* to describe the ultimate result of protracted divorce litigation. Sadly, I have learned that little of this is hyperbole. Divorce litigation becomes like the island of Dr. Moreau in H. G. Wells's novel. The abused and horrified litigants want to row their boat away from that island at any cost. I was no different. I wanted nothing more than to put this entire experience behind me and get on with my life. I had grown weary of writing this book, until I would meet another man who had suffered the same way I had. Suddenly, the old passion to address these issues would return.

DIVORCE LITIGATION IS A UNIQUE phenomenon in our culture. When someone is sick, our society usually offers some means of care. Often that care extends to their families as well. The sick individual reaches out to professionals who arrive with their skills and training at the ready, prepared to solve the problem. When illness afflicts a marriage, however, the professionals who arrive on the scene often are there to prolong the bleeding, not to stop it. To be pulled into the American family law system in most states is like being tied to the back of a pickup truck and dragged down a gravel road late at night. No one can hear your cries and complaints, and it is not over until they say it is over.

Early in my own divorce proceedings I came upon men who told me that the corrosiveness and complexity of their divorces had forced them to give up. They "wrote off" not only their first marriages, but their children as well. Many went on to remarry. The chance to "make things right" meant starting another family. I could never, ever comprehend how a man could abandon his child in this way. However, as my own proceedings went on, and the recriminations became more severe, I began to appreciate these men, and some women as well, better than I imagined possible. I have sat with men whose hearts are filled with love for their children. Before their divorce there had never been any doubt of that love or their abilities as parents. Then divorce lawyers entered the picture to do what many of them do best: destroy an innocent parent's reputation and their bond with their children. Therefore, lawyers, along with ineffectual judges who do little to curb such destructive forces in American family law, are a principal focus of this book.

Family law in most states has become its own preserve, one in which litigants come and go while the principal players remain the same. Those players, not the families whose fates are determined by this system, are the ones who profit from protecting the status quo. We have, I believe, a system designed to line the pockets of these principals. Anything that results in effective conflict resolution, protection of both parents' rights, and, most important, a healthy environment for the children of divorce is a happy accident. The problem lies not only with antagonistic lawyers who perpetuate conflict but also with the judges who sit idly by and do nothing to rein them in.

However, this book is not a blanket indictment of all attorneys and the legal profession. I will cite by name some of the truly constructive and decent men and women I have encountered during my own proceedings. (Unfortunately, under the current system, decency and humanity often work against family law attorneys.) Nor do I mean to imply that a legal divorce is always an unsafe option when a relationship has degenerated beyond repair. There are times when dissolving a marriage is the best decision a couple can make. American taxpayers, however, continue to fund a system that turns a sensitive and private decision into a destructive process that leaves few unscathed. If getting out of your marriage is good for both you and your estranged spouse, it ought to be easier to achieve. The truth is that we maintain a system in which destroying one's ex-spouse, not effectively resolving conflict, is the order of the day.

WHAT FOLLOWS WILL DISAPPOINT those who hoped to find a gossipy, salacious tale of a show business marriage gone bad. Tabloid publications have already put out enough such stories about my protracted divorce and ensuing custody battle. I do not feel compelled to set that record straight. Think what you will. What stories someone's own imagination can come up with will be far more satisfying, in that regard, than the truth. Necessity demands that I include some of the particulars of my own case, but only those germane to the book's purpose. However, you will come away disappointed if you hope to find a bitter, angry attack against my ex-wife. When I write of my own experience, I present my side of the story and interpretation of what occurred. As all divorce litigants should eventually realize, attacking the other party is not in anyone's interest, especially when children are involved. It does no good for a parent to bury their ex-spouse on the pages of a book, so I reserve my attacks for the family law system, specifically the Los Angeles County system where my own case was adjudicated.

Most important, this book is not an attempt to escape responsibility for my own actions. I do not ask anyone to believe that this is all someone else's fault. Much of the trouble I found myself in came about as the result of a series of mistakes and bad judgments I made throughout both my marriage and divorce. Knowing what I do now about myself and my ex-wife, about our approaches to life, our personalities, what makes us happy, even something as simple as where we wanted to live, it might have been in everyone's best interest if we'd never married. But that kind of thinking is pointless. We did marry, and in the process we, like so many others, ignored signs of what lay ahead. I made choices that led to the place where I am now. In the pages that follow I accept full responsibility for them.

Because of the scope of the problem this book explores, the issues raised could never be fully articulated through my own case alone. Therefore I have chosen three men to share their own stories and perspectives. All of them have changed their names and the specifics of their identities. One of the subjects is an amalgam of different individuals' stories. Although I believe that to omit the particulars of my own case would be counterproductive to the book's purpose, it has never been my goal to embarrass anyone in the process. Adding some of my own experiences to those of my contributors proved to be the most effective way to explore key issues while leaving everyone's dignity largely intact.

MANY READERS, ESPECIALLY the attorneys and other professionals who play integral roles in the family law system, will automatically dismiss this book as nothing more than the grumblings of a bitter and angry man. Rather than falling prey to a corrupt system, they will say I am the victim of my own poor choices and brought all this on myself by marrying the wrong woman, hiring the wrong lawyer, or through my own boorish behavior. After all, I should have known I stood a good chance of ending up inside a divorce court. Half of all marriages end in divorce, and Hollywood marriages fare even worse. My time of being chained behind the pickup truck of the legal system was my own bad luck. *Everyone* knows little good ever comes out of our legal system, usually varying degrees of bad. I should have had the good sense to avoid it at all costs. Besides, my situation is, in these critics' eyes, an anomaly. It is the exception, not the rule. I could have chosen a course that would have shortened the legal process and lessened my pain. I could have given up. Caved. Others have. I should have as well. Instead, these same critics would say my persistence only made things worse for myself.

I agree that I did make things worse for myself. Foolishly, I walked into a courtroom with the expectation that I would be given some equitable rights regarding my daughter. I ignored the less than subtle message that tells noncustodial parents, especially fathers, to abandon such hopes and face the realities of this system. Walk away, we're told. Accept your fate as your penance for the poor choices you've made. Write off this failed family as the price of learning difficult lessons. The longer you hold out for what should be the right of every parent, the more expensive and painful the process becomes.

Indeed, I went through very bitter litigation. But I did not have a contentious divorce proceeding because I sought alimony or other financial concessions from my ex-wife. My litigation did not involve unreasonable personal demands about where my ex could live or whether she could move on with her life. Alternately, I did not seek to move my daughter to London or Paris. I had a contentious divorce because I wanted a meaningful custody of my daughter. I refused to settle for becoming a "Disney Dad," one whose role is nothing more than outings to theme parks once or twice a month. Instead, I wanted to share the joys and responsibilities of raising my daughter. I wanted to be a real father, and the system punished me for that. Ultimately, I refused to give in, and for a period, I prevailed.

If the circumstances of my case had been truly anomalous, I likely would have taken my lumps and got on with my life. I would not have written this book if I felt that my experiences were isolated. However, I have seen the other broken lives and destruction that this system leaves in its wake. I have even had attorneys, in a fleeting moment of candor, admit that the system is terribly flawed. I am not stating that every divorce proceeding is the same. Nor am I suggesting that most divorce lawyers and family law judges are at best inept or at worst corrupt. There is, however, enough injustice, inefficiency, and corruption within the system to compel us as a society to closely examine what is being perpetrated on innocent men and women, funded by our tax dollars. As you read my story and the stories of others that follow, I believe you will reach this same conclusion.

SOME PEOPLE WILL, NO DOUBT, criticize me for tilting this book so much toward my own dilemma as opposed to that of my daughter. However, due to restrictions set by court orders, as well as a desire not to expose my child to any further unnecessary scrutiny, an open and frank discussion of my observations of my daughter's experiences is, to an extent, better left alone. My relationship with my daughter might have been a casualty of parental alienation, aided and abetted by the Los Angeles family law system. As I have suffered, so has she, in my opinion. I have included only as much of my daughter's reality as I saw fit.

I have seen the psychological toll that divorce litigation takes on people. These victims are not an isolated few, hidden away from the rest of society, as was often the case some generations ago. Today, more than half of all marriages end in divorce, and the damages are not limited to the couples themselves. The aftereffects of divorce seep into all of society. This phenomenon of acrimonious divorce litigation exacts an incalculable psychological and emotional toll not only on the litigants but on innocent bystanders as well. Like any social issue, there is a cost we all bear, spiritually as well as financially.

Among the several topics that my contributors and I will examine in this book are:

- Prenuptial agreements and how couples can attempt to preemptively protect themselves, their respective extended families, and, of course, their children from the unnecessary pain of divorce litigation.

- How to approach the ultimate decision to file for divorce, specifically in both high- and low-conflict divorces. We explore the question of when, as well as how, to file.

- Divorce strategies and assessments for couples with above average, average, and below average assets.

- Selecting an attorney. Is word of mouth all it's cracked up to be?

- Private mediation versus going to trial.

- Observations on judges, forensic accountants, custody evaluations and evaluators, collateral witnesses, child psychologists, and other court-appointed therapists.

- An examination of actual custody/visitation strategies. What should your time with your child be like? How does the inevitable passage of time affect you and your growing child?

- The newly divorced parent's life and the hopeful prayer of constructive co-parenting.

- The political influences on current family law. How the political apparatus of lawyers, judges, and feminist groups assaults fatherhood and impacts custody.

I have been through some of the worst of contentious divorce litigation. I have lost some proceedings that seemed important at the time, but I prevailed in many others. Wisdom has urged me to walk away from this experience and count my blessings. But I have chosen to return to it, to examine it again, and to share with you not only my thoughts but those of others, as well. A book is not a Pollock painting; its web of facts and feelings must be arranged in an ordered way. To that end, I have enlisted the aid of Mark Tabb, who helped me with the research, organization, and writing of what follows.

This book is entitled *A Promise to Ourselves*. And it is in fulfillment of that promise that I offer to all divorced fathers, to all parents, the dreams and nightmares, the insights and ultimate lessons of my own story.

1

Even the Deepest Feelings

O<small>N A SUNDAY MORNING</small> in January of 2001, I stood on
a cold Manhattan street with a movie crew as we prepared
to shoot the first scenes of a film I was directing. For me,
this was a dream come true, not only because I was directing for the first time, but also because of the incredible cast
we had assembled for the project, including Anthony Hopkins, Jennifer Love Hewitt, Dan Aykroyd, Kim Cattrall, and
Barry Miller. Pete Dexter wrote the script and Bill Condon
did the rewrite, just prior to winning the Oscar for *Gods and
Monsters*. And as if all of that weren't enough, we were going
to make the film during my favorite season in my favorite
place. Later that winter, heavy snow fell on New York during our shooting schedule, like the winters of my childhood.
I was elated by the possibilities.

Yet the joy of the moment was mitigated by a painful un-
certainty hanging over my personal life. My wife of seven
years had packed her things from our New York home and

had moved back to Los Angeles a few weeks earlier. We talked in the ensuing weeks with words that vacillated between animosity and a seemingly perfunctory hope of reconciliation. Even as I faced the reality that we had grown apart, I also believed that our relationship might be salvaged. Less than a month before our separation I found my wife distressed over a minor health problem. Instinctively, I put my arms around her and tried to assure her that everything would be all right. No matter what she faced, I would be there for her. My desire to care for her was reflexive and immediate. I had been with this woman for more than ten years. She was my wife, my friend, and the mother of my only child and I wanted to make her troubles go away. Four weeks later she was gone.

Even though all of these thoughts swirled in my head as I stood on East Fifty-third Street, preparing to roll the camera for our first shot of the day, I tried to focus on the job at hand. Suddenly, a man I assumed was an extra walked up to me, smiling, and asked if I was Alec Baldwin. I smiled back and said yes. His whole demeanor then changed as he pressed an envelope against my chest. "This is for you," he said. "Oh, yeah," he added as he walked away, "I'm a big fan of your work." I opened the envelope, which was filled with legal documents. Although I had asked my wife to delay any legal action until after the film shoot was over, she had served me with formal separation papers right there on the set of the movie. Our marriage was officially over.

I can honestly say that a part of me never saw it coming. Although I knew I was unhappy and I was certain that my wife was as well, talking about divorce is one thing, actually carrying it out is quite another. Even when I had contemplated the dissolution of my marriage over the past several months, I still believed we had something worth fighting for. I found it hard to believe that this was the end. I also found it equally hard to believe that my ex-wife would choose to dive back into the civil court system that only a few short years earlier had nearly destroyed her.

The deep feelings of love that sweep you into a marriage don't die overnight. The process is often slow and, typically, painful. Understanding how these feelings die can be as painful as the loss itself. When relationships end, some people naturally reflect upon what led them to that point. Others seek to affix blame. Therefore, some find it necessary to renounce their feelings, thereby nullifying everything that came before. That is when you hear people say, "I never loved her." Or, "I never really cared for him." This nullification is nothing but a lie some people tell themselves. Litigants will say in open court that "my husband was Saddam Hussein," to which I once heard a judge reply, "Well then, why did you marry Saddam Hussein?" These litigants and their attorneys find it convenient to burn the couple's past down to the ground and seek to paint a picture of their ex-spouse that is wildly distorted. Hopefully, a judge will see through this. I, however, was incapable of denying what I had once felt. Therefore, I looked back in an attempt to understand what had attracted me to my ex-wife in the beginning and how our relationship had failed.

We have all heard the many angles on how one should choose a spouse and, thus, increase the chances of a happy marriage. Some say a woman marries a man hoping to change him, while a man marries a woman hoping she will never change. Others say men should look to their girlfriend's mother, a woman to her husband's father, because that is what your spouse will become in twenty-five years. They say never marry a woman who is close with her father, or a man who is close with his mother, as you are unlikely to ever measure up to that figure in their life. I suppose that I had some prejudices, fantasies, and hang-ups of my own going into my marriage. To a degree, I wanted a wife who was, in some ways, like my mother and not at all like her in others. Oddly enough, however, it was my father, and the role he had played in my life, that had more of an impact on my marriage than anyone or anything else.

MY FATHER TAUGHT SCHOOL for twenty-eight years in Massapequa, Long Island. He'd dropped out of Syracuse Law School to take an entry-level teaching position in a newly formed school district. His uncle told him that a respectable career as a school administrator would be his, with a little effort. But my father never left the classroom. Not only did he not become an administrator, he never even became a department head. It wasn't that my father was a bad teacher; quite the opposite. The students adored him. Twice the student body dedicated their yearbook to him while he was still living and active, an honor normally given to those retired or dead.

My father refused to play the political games necessary to advance. One man in particular could have made my dad's life unimaginably easier if my father had just played ball. But my father refused. He didn't think it was right. Self-respect and integrity were always front and center with my dad, a former marine. "Judge me by my merits" was his attitude. And he never attained the level of success he might have because of it.

My relationship with my father evolved in the years after I left home. He became a more essential advisor and mentor to me, someone whose judgment I trusted almost implicitly. He supported my decision to pursue a career in acting in New York after I left George Washington University. I found his advice invaluable as I moved further into the entertainment industry, where men like my father were few and far between. Just as I was making the transition from New York to Los Angeles, my father died suddenly, of cancer, at the age of fifty-five. His passing left a huge void in my life. Over the next few years I began to actively, even unconsciously, search for someone who could fill his role, not as a parent, but as a trusted ally in a cutthroat business. Little did I know that I would find just that in a beauty-queen-turned-movie-star from Athens, Georgia.

Kim made a quick ascent up the Hollywood ladder in the late 1970s and early 1980s. She went from modeling and commercials to television and feature films in a relatively short time. When we met on the set of a film in 1990, she'd already established herself as a major star. Although she'd achieved a great deal of success in a difficult business, she did not allow the industry to consume her. She loved movies but was rarely a part of that world on a social basis. Like my father, she refused to play the games necessary to gain any advantage in her career. Kim could have married the head of the studio, network, or talent agency, the Oscar-winning star or producer. Instead she chose to allow her body of work to speak for itself. She felt she should be judged by her merits, nothing more. It was this quality, more than any other, that most attracted me to her.

Prior to meeting my ex-wife, I had often walked away from intimate relationships after about eighteen months.

That is not to say that I would not return out of some combination of love, pity, and/or loneliness. After about a year and a half, however, I was ready to move on. My relationship with my ex-wife was no different. We met in April of 1990, and by November of the following year, almost like clockwork, I once again felt lingering incompatibility issues rising up. I noticed major differences in our attitudes toward family and friends, our careers and acting itself, our places in the community and the public eye. For all of her image as a go-it-alone iconoclast, I discovered Kim rarely did anything without the advice of a team of people. The more powerful her agents, publicists, and business managers were, the more she believed their advice should be heeded. Kim did not necessarily wish to socialize with important Hollywood figures, yet she rarely made a move without consulting one. This reliance upon highly paid professionals would prove to be a major factor contributing to my eventual divorce difficulties.

As I hit the eighteen-month mark in this relationship, once again I struggled with how I could care for this person and yet, at times, feel so alone. Unlike before, however, I resolved that I would not walk away. This time, I would stay and try to make it work. I believed with all my heart that if I kept my focus on my own issues, the rest would take care of itself. "Love suffereth long, and is kind," I was told. I chose to believe that. I pushed through these feelings and stayed. Less than one year later my resolve would be put to the test when Kim, upon the advice of her agent, pulled out of a movie and was sued by the film's producers.

In the spring of 1992, the plaintiffs alleged that Kim had agreed to star in a movie called *Boxing Helena*. Kim asked for full written disclosure of the amount of nudity and physical contact with other actors that the part required. She counterclaimed that the producers did not satisfactorily provide this information. Therefore she walked away under the terms of the Screen Actors Guild contract. Furthermore, her new agents assured her that they would "make this thing go away." Instead, Kim was sued for millions of dollars and lost. At the onset of the lawsuit, Kim's entertainment contract lawyer tried to convince her to settle out of court. However, Kim wanted no part of it. She refused to settle a case when she believed she had done nothing wrong. Like my father, she only wanted what was fair. Ironically, this principled stubbornness set off a chain of events that strained our relationship even before we married. Although I recognized this in hindsight, at the time I supported Kim in her decision and I trusted the court would vindicate her.

Rather than protect her, the system left her physically, emotionally, and financially broken. From the start, the plaintiffs' lawyer, a vicious, menacing woman named Patty Glaser, posited the case as a showdown between a rich, privileged movie star and struggling filmmakers who had to work hard for whatever meager success they had achieved. Kim, Glaser said, was like the pretty girl in school who bypassed the rules with impunity. Nothing could be further from the truth. Kim had a very professional work ethic, but the jury bought it. Adding to the injury, Kim's agents had originally been named as codefendants. Halfway through the proceedings they successfully petitioned the court to be dismissed from the case, yet the judge inexplicably did not disclose this ruling to the jury. That meant the go-it-alone Kim bore the sole financial responsibility for the eventual nine-million-dollar judgment.

After the verdict, the judge, Judith Chirlin, strode across the courtroom and hugged the plaintiffs in full view of the entire proceeding. Even Kim's veteran attorney, Howard Weitzman, was aghast. In subsequent depositions, one juror said that nine million dollars was little more than a "parking ticket" to someone like Kim.

The lawsuit and judgment exacted a steep emotional, as well as financial, price. Los Angeles is a town completely consumed by perception. The woman who was wealthier and more famous than I was when I met her in 1990 was now bankrupt and humiliated three years later. After the jury handed down its decision, Kim and I returned to her home in Los Angeles, where the stress and losses of the trial took their toll. One evening she collapsed under the weight, sobbing on the deck beside her pool. Prior to the verdict in the trial, some friends had encouraged me to end this relationship. They told me that she was self-destructive. Watching her lying there, however, I thought to myself, *How can I leave her now?* Kim was not one for self-pity. She would cry for the poor, the homeless, for abused animals, but never for herself. Like my father, her suffering came because she had stood on principle. However, this time I had the resources to do something to help. Soon after, I proposed and Kim accepted. Perhaps she needed security, support, and financial resources to help her navigate the whitewater she was about to encounter while appealing her verdict and living under bankruptcy jurisdiction. Perhaps while crushed by an unfair verdict, she needed to believe that someone would help her, would stand by her, and take her side. I wanted to be that person. On August 19, 1993, we were married.

* * *

WHEN RELATIONSHIPS BEGIN, romance ought to be the order of the day. The first couple of years should be a time of candlelight and intimate conversation, travel and entertainment. A time to deepen your understanding of and appreciation for each other. My relationship with my ex-wife was no different, at least during our first two years together. Life held no stress, no entanglements. We would travel to New York or London, or pass the time reading scripts that producers had sent our way. Life seemed easy, and I enjoyed Kim's company enormously.

Everything changed with the lawsuit and Kim's subsequent bankruptcy proceedings. Our life became an endless procession of lawyers delivering a ceaseless chorus of bad news. Lawyers advised Kim to declare federal bankruptcy, but what she thought would bring relief only unleashed more pain. We entered a new phase, with attorneys intruding into every aspect of our daily lives as a bankruptcy trustee took full control of her seized assets. Kim's own bankruptcy attorney would call nearly every day regarding decisions that had to be made. Kim did not have the emotional reserves to deal with any of it. Someone had to give some direction, and that fell to me. On top of this, Kim engaged more lawyers and appealed the judgment against her. She was, some time later, granted a "reversal without direction," which legally granted a new trial yet no return of her money.

The ongoing bankruptcy ordeal came packed with inexplicable malice and bad faith. The worst of it occurred one rainy afternoon when the bankruptcy trustee ordered the seizure of Kim's personal and professional property from her office. Sheriff's deputies literally stormed into the building and took everything. Her files, the memorabilia she had collected from her own films and those of people she admired, antique furniture, electronic equipment, and every last paper clip were flung into the back of a pickup truck, uncovered, and hauled away in the rain. Many of the items they seized were irreplaceable and much of it was damaged or never seen again.

Kim was depressed, unemployed, and not easy to be around. Her treatment in the press did not help matters. On New Year's Day of 1995 the *New York Times* Sunday business section ran a front-page article about people who used bankruptcy protection to avoid paying their debts. The piece featured Kim's litigation. Accompanying the piece was a photograph of my then home in East Hampton, New York. The article referred to it as Kim's "Hampton estate" and implied that she lived in luxury while evading her creditors. This, of course, was blatantly false. The house was a premarital asset of mine, which I had bought for a small sum in 1987. The article was unfair to the point of ridiculous. Such articles were typical of how Kim was treated in the press during this period. Many mornings throughout 1993 and 1994, Kim's assistant and I would comb the newspapers for unfavorable depictions of Kim and her case to shield her from them.

As all of this churned around us, I found myself growing more and more frustrated with the way business was conducted in Hollywood. Anger seethed inside me over the way my wife was being treated. Her agent and others, who should have stood beside her, scurried away to protect themselves, leaving her to face this all on her own. Kim was accused of refusing to honor a contract, yet I had been on the other end when a studio chose not to honor a contract with me. The unwritten code in Hollywood, however, is that a performer can never sue the studios, not if you expect to ever work in movies again. Early on in my career, as I slowly worked my way up, I was filled with gratitude for the opportunities I received. Yet once I had moved up that ladder, I began to see another side of Hollywood. I believe there is more greed and dishonor in the movie business than anywhere else. In terms of honor and dignity, the illegal drug business looks like the Boy Scouts by comparison.

The pain and frustration in my work, combined with the stresses in my marriage, created the worst of all circumstances. At work, I was disappointed by a system whose games I now refused to play. I came home to share in self-pity and bitterness over the hand that we had been dealt. By 1994, the bankruptcy attorney would call with her daily report, and at that point, we had devised a shorthand. I would ask, "Was it a ten or a nine today?" This was a measure of how badly Kim had been treated during the proceeding, ten being the worst. Most days were either a nine or a ten.

After nearly two years of this, the issues we faced as a couple grew larger and more pronounced. I had been in other relationships and recognized the look that people get when they would prefer that you were not around. Kim hardly looked me in the eye anymore and seemed always to be talking to me over her shoulder.

The *New York Times* piece on Kim's bankruptcy ran on New Year's Day, 1995. Kim was once again made to look callous and irresponsible in a way that, under the slightest examination, was clearly untrue. Kim was livid. We were scheduled to fly that night to Lima to begin shooting a documentary on endangered exotic birds of the Peruvian rain forest. I had hoped that working on this project together would help our marriage, but once again, the case overshadowed everything. Kim did not want to go on the trip, partly because of a tantrum I had thrown over the *Times* piece. The documentary, which I had helped to organize, appeared to be ruined. Ultimately, Kim relented and we headed to Peru. We did not talk much, although the project proved to be exhilarating. We flew home somewhat renewed. And then we discovered Kim was pregnant with our daughter.

WE WERE STANDING in her bathroom in her house in Los Angeles: Kim, myself, and Kim's then assistant. Kim said she had something to tell me. She seemed lost in thought, bordering on grim. Her assistant had a slightly woeful smile on her face. Kim said she was pregnant. A moment that one would have imagined, during all of your lifetime leading up until now, would be a cause for unprecedented joy was more like someone telling you that they had wrecked your car. Or that your house had been flooded. We all just stood there while Kim talked of her doubts about me and our marriage. She was, however, determined to move forward with having the child, in spite of our current state of disconnect. Her assistant managed to sneak glances at me that seemed pitying, as if to say, "How sad to have this moment in your life play out this way." I suppose that, in hindsight, the alienation from my daughter began that afternoon, before she was even born.

I HAD COMMITTED to make a film in New York in the spring of 1995. After all we had been through, I was not automatically inclined to attempt to get out of that contract.

However, when I had found out that Kim was pregnant, I asked the producers to release me from the project so I could remain home with my new family. True to form, they refused and threatened to sue me. Kim was due to deliver our baby in late October, just six weeks before her forty-second birthday. During her pregnancy, I would travel back to Los Angeles frequently, but no one greeted me with any of the protocol of the expectant father. Kim was having a baby, not me. I was reminded of that constantly. I wrote this off as the fears and doubts of an expectant mother, but it all seemed wrong. There was never any talk of bringing Kim's mother or mine or any of our siblings, most of whom had children, to L.A. to participate in Kim's care. It was go-it-alone time again. As the due date drew near, there was some warmth and even some closeness. But the overall experience left me wondering if this was how it was supposed to be.

After my daughter was born, like many new fathers, I felt an almost instinctual need to work harder to make us more secure. My film career was never robust, but 1996 proved to be a good one for me and for Kim as well. I shot *Ghosts of Mississippi* in Los Angeles, and Kim shot *L.A. Confidential* there at around the same time. Next, I went to Alberta, Canada, to shoot *The Edge*, with Anthony Hopkins. My daughter was just shy of a year old, but my wife complained about putting her on a plane to see me. The flight to Calgary was just over two hours, but Kim came there with my daughter only once. I worked what was an unusually tough schedule and flew to L.A. nearly every other weekend. Kim complained about my being away, but I maintained that one of us had to work. Then, suddenly, *L.A. Confidential* was released in 1997 and the film was a critical success. Soon thereafter, Kim was nominated for an Oscar, and as if in a dream, she won in early 1998. Five years after her loss in civil court, Kim had a beautiful daughter, an Oscar, and the opportunity to earn back nearly all of the money she had lost in court.

Kim had been restored to the place she longed to be and starred in two films between 1998 and 1999. I clearly sensed that by then I had outlived my usefulness to her. I accompanied her to Africa in the fall of 1998, but I was really just the third nanny in the rotation. In 1999, I went to Montreal to work and she to Toronto. By the fall of 1999, my daughter was ready for preschool. I commuted to Toronto nearly every weekend to see Ireland. No provisions were made for a tutor, or for any type of academic program, as Ireland turned four years old. My daughter would essentially visit her mother on the movie set and then spend the remainder of the day sitting in an expensive hotel suite, reading books or watching television with a nanny.

I did not graduate Phi Beta Kappa from Harvard, but I wanted my daughter's educational needs to be addressed with some real care and deliberation. We were now approaching the end of the road. I urged my wife to move to New York to put my daughter into school, as I did not want my child raised in Los Angeles. By 2000, we lived in eastern Long Island. My wife complained, nearly every day, that the weather there was making my daughter sick. I countered that my daughter was sick on a regular basis because she was in school. Like all children, she was building the immune system that would protect her for the rest of her life. I took off nearly all of 2000, working for only six weeks that year, in order to drive my daughter to school each day. Often I would go to the school to pick up my daughter's missed assignments, only to see other kids with symptoms that had kept my daughter home. One teacher told me that her rule was that if the child does not have a fever, convince her to attend school. My wife would hear none of it. She threatened daily to head back to Los Angeles. I reminded her that Los Angeles, with its mythic air pollution and over-crowding, was no environmental Eden by any stretch. It was ostensibly over this issue that, on December 8, we had the argument that ended our marriage. I moved out of the house. We had very little contact. I wanted to see Ireland, but suddenly, as the semester ended, Kim was off to Los Angeles and, as I later found out, contacted an attorney to begin divorce proceedings.

SOON THEREAFTER, I WAS DRIVING down a road in East Hampton when it hit me: that unmistakable and shuddering wave that comes over you when you own the truth that your marriage is over. Now you are like all of the other millions who have failed, or at least feel they have, at something so personal. Something that meant so much to you and that you tried so hard to keep alive is dead. I pulled my car to the side of the road, snow falling all around me. I let out sounds I did not know were in me. I cried and thought how helpless I felt, helplessness having been, in my lifetime, the most demoralizing feeling of all.

MY WIFE HAD FINALLY STOPPED pretending to listen to my opinion about my daughter, or anything else, and gone back to L.A. with no regard for any of my rights, or those of my child to see her father. I had loved this woman, once. As things would grow more contentious and bitter, I wondered how she could behave this way. Eventually, my disbelief would become immeasurable. I asked my therapist, an intelligent, mature, kind woman, a wife and mother herself, "What am I supposed to take from this?" Her answer was, "Now you've learned one of life's most painful lessons: that even the deepest feelings don't last forever."

2

Let the Games Begin

I walked toward Bob Kaufman, across the driveway of his spectacular Malibu cliffside compound. Kaufman, who had been introduced to me by a New York attorney named Sanford Lotwin, had agreed to take my case and, after I paid him a retainer of $25,000, he wanted me to come to his home to meet with two of his associates. My case was to be heard in a Los Angeles courtroom.

PRIOR TO THAT MEETING in January of 2001, I had met Lotwin in Manhattan. A tall, distinguished man who maintained an impeccable reputation as a divorce attorney in New York, Lotwin sat with me at the Plaza Athénée hotel, accompanied by his associate, Sheila Riesel. Riesel and Lotwin peppered me with questions as people, flush with the holiday spirit, churned through the hotel bar. It was December of 2000 and before the 9/11 attacks. As others were Christmas shopping and on their way to holiday parties, I sat while these two strangers probed, respectfully, about the circumstances of the end of my marriage.

Both Lotwin and Riesel were low-key but assured. At that time, they insisted that I file a restraining order to prevent my then wife from leaving New York with my daughter. This was the only way to proceed, Lotwin stressed, or she could file in California and claim that we were "co-domiciled," meaning we actually lived in both places. I would have to spend a lot of time and money in an attempt to change jurisdictions and still would probably not succeed. Riesel, one of the few lawyers I met during the entire process who actually had a soul, was calm and clear. "You must stop her from leaving," she said. "Or the case will be heard in California, which is not so good for you." The next day, I phoned my ex-wife. She stated, forcefully, that she and the child wanted to "go home." She condemned me for "forcing" them to remain in New York. I ignored Riesel and Lotwin's advice and caved. My daughter traveled with her mother to my in-laws for Christmas, then on to L.A. A couple of weeks later, I was served with papers on West Fifty-third Street.

Bob Kaufman, a bearded, bearish man, ushered me onto the grounds of his incredible home. At one point, he asked, "Where are you staying while you're in town?" I told him the name of a hotel in Santa Monica. He replied, "I have a guesthouse right over there. You're welcome to stay here, if you like." I had spoken to Kaufman once on the phone and met him less than thirty seconds ago, and already I was houseguest material. Inside, seated at the kitchen table, were two younger men. Kaufman sat, and thus began the next major lesson in my divorce education. Kaufman asked questions. Everyone remained quiet and grim. They wanted the story, without the varnish. As I told it, they would grunt and nod. Sometimes they glared at each other, as if every painful or humiliating moment I recounted were their own. Within minutes, Kaufman had the demeanor of someone very angry and dangerous. He was completely transformed from the genial fellow in the driveway. Kaufman muttered some opinions to the others and they, in turn, responded or asked questions. Kaufman is a major Los Angeles divorce attorney, and rather than put my mind at ease, he basically scared the hell out of me.

In the weeks that followed, Kaufman wanted meetings with me to devise a strategy. I was working and not always available, but I think it is safe to say that I was avoiding him. As my ex-wife had during her proceedings in 1993, I had quickly grown to mistrust civil attorneys and the system they represented. Kaufman wanted to get started, to take depositions and begin tearing into the other side. That is what he did. I was tentative about it all. As ludicrous as it seems, I believe I rightly fell into a category of people who fired their attorneys because they were too mean. They were excessively combative and lacking in the skills needed to stem the conflict, let alone resolve it. Soon thereafter, Kaufman and I parted ways. Suddenly, after a few short months, it was already time to go shopping for my second divorce lawyer.

Although I had many friends who themselves were divorced, with few exceptions, most were reluctant to talk about their experiences. Once a judge issued their final orders, they were anxious to put this part of their lives behind them. I understood, from personal experience, that you want to bury the unpleasantness and move on as fast as you possibly can. No doubt my friends were empathetic, but my experience brought back their own pain. Often this made me reluctant to even broach the subject. Therefore, I did not ask them for advice or to recommend an attorney.

That is not to say that I had any shortage of people offering their help or opinions. Since we live in a culture of divorce, seemingly everywhere I went, I ran into people who had a brother or sister or some guy who worked in the cubicle next to theirs who knew an attorney I should meet. *"My friend Debbie had an awful divorce and she used so-and-so and he was just fantastic,"* someone would tell me, sounding as if they were recommending a caterer for a party. Eventually, I would come to realize that it seemed oxymoronic to have an awful divorce and a lovable lawyer. Most well-regarded divorce lawyers are merely the most aggressive or diabolical. Seeking some degree of humanity in a divorce attorney can lead to a lot of unnecessary pain.

This is one of the most critical decisions one can make in this process, yet many people approach it without the information they may need to make an informed choice. I came to this with little to no experience. As a child, I knew hardly anyone who was divorced. In the middle-class world of my childhood, it was either still a taboo or was simply too costly for most to consider practically. Therefore, I simply consulted my own entertainment attorney, and his recommendation led me to that first Plaza Athénée meeting. This reliance upon such incestuous referrals within a particular legal community, where lawyers recommend one another, can lead to serious problems. The same is true for word-of-mouth recommendations from friends or associates who have no actual experience with the process. They can only tell you how Debbie's divorce went.

Both the "legal community" and word-of-mouth paths are flawed because they ask the wrong questions. Instead of inquiring whether someone "knows the name of a good divorce lawyer," you need to examine the kind of divorce litigation you face and find an attorney best suited to your needs. When my ex-wife and I separated, I did not know a forensic accountant from a special master. I had no idea what a custody evaluation was or what "divorce commissioners" did or what to expect in the weeks and months ahead. I wrongly believed my attorney would effectively guide me through the process, educating me along the way. In my experience, however, they obscured or downplayed much of the unpleasantness I was to face. They skimped on the education part and insisted I leave the messy details to them. They provided little information, and even much of that was irrelevant to the questions I had asked. They were inside a system, an inefficient, corrupt, amoral system, and they wanted to be left to work that system with as little interference from me as possible.

Ironically, some of the most helpful advice I found came from an unlikely source: those who have gone through multiple divorces. Someone who has had more than one encounter with the process, one with a clear head and cold eye, can be invaluable. But it is somewhere else entirely that one's preparation for these events should begin. That is with family care professionals.

I recommend individual litigants consult a family care professional who conducts divorced co-parenting sessions and/or classes. This is critical. Find a therapist who has worked with other couples, preferably from a variety of backgrounds, but one who will not be involved in your litigation. Discuss with them the particulars of your relationship with your estranged spouse and children. What issues will likely emerge or have already emerged? They may then be able to tell you whether you and your spouse will be able to mediate questions of custody, or whether you face some form of custody fight. These therapists may not have all of the answers you want. However, they are generally more concerned with the welfare of the participants than any attorney will ever be. When they speak of the "best interests of the child," they are more likely to mean it. This is an essential step to take, early on, to prepare you for what lies ahead.

Arguably, the least contentious and fairest divorces are where there is little or no money and/or where no children are involved. Couples with limited assets to divide and no custody questions to settle move through the family law system more quickly. However, once children enter the picture, the potential for protracted conflict increases exponentially, as does the cost of litigation. Studies show that the average cost of divorce in the United States runs between fifteen and thirty thousand dollars, with the process dragging out at least one year. Most of that money is funneled directly to lawyers. If the case cannot be mediated and ends up in court, the figure is raised significantly. A two-day trial can cost as much as twenty-five thousand dollars. Mediation and arbitration are less expensive but can still average from five to ten thousand dollars. Of course, the battle between couples with deep pockets and lingering, unresolved personal issues becomes the Super Bowl for divorce attorneys.

Subsequently, divorce is now a $28 billion industry in the United States.[1]

The average person does not have large reserves of liquid assets they can tap to pay legal fees. However, they may have one asset that can be converted into cash: their home. This is one of the earliest painful realities one can encounter in the divorce process. Lawyers tell their clients that dividing the assets of the divorced couple will unavoidably impact the lifestyle of both parties. Unless you are wealthy enough to simply shrug off the numbers, selling your home to pay property settlements with your ex or, worse yet, to access cash to pay legal fees, is one of the more catastrophic moments of the process. Running through asset statements with your attorney, you may come across that look from him that implies, "Well everybody knows that when you get divorced you have to sell your house." If both spouses lack the cash to buy out the other's half of the home, the house must be sold and the equity divided between the two. Of course, children are uprooted as well, potentially leaving behind schools, friends, and neighbors, perhaps even family. Parents, not all of them wealthy, who had once shouldered the expense of private schools must suddenly seek neighborhoods where better public schools, in combination with more affordable housing, are their new, fragile reality. I have had countless people tell me how they lost homes, entire businesses, and relationships directly due to the costs of divorce. The end result is that couples that come into litigation as middle-class homeowners depart significantly poorer, renting apartments

[1]Leah Hoffman, "To Have and to Hold On To," *Forbes*, November 7, 2006, www.forbes.com/personalfinance/2006/11/07/divorce-costs-legal-biz-cx_lh_1107legaldivorce.html (accessed May 19, 2008).

or condos that fall below the standard they once took for granted.

THE FIRST THING you are required to do in divorce proceedings is to provide your "financials." You reveal, to complete strangers, how much you are worth, on paper, and how it can be accessed and divided to pay your obligations. Initially, the purpose of this is obvious and the timeliness of it is understandable. Money must start to flow from one party to the other in order to pay for children's doctor bills, clothes, and tuition. The other result, however, is that your lawyers know precisely how much money you have. I reached a point where I honestly imagined that my attorneys had calculated a number in their minds, a number that represented a percentage of my net worth and that this figure had become the firm's surreptitious goal. At times, I thought I could hear their voices, wafting all the way from their Century City offices, saying, "This is the number we've got to hit in this case." It was a number they knew I had and they knew how to get.

I encourage people to do the very thing that lawyers hate most: settle your case through wholly private mediation. Agreements reached through purely private mediation almost always prove more ethical than what results from going to court. The two sides tend to reach agreement more thoughtfully and comprehensively, fairly and even self-critically. In wholly private mediation, you negotiate an acceptable divorce agreement with the help of a neutral third party who knows the law in your jurisdiction. Mediators help the two sides communicate but do not make decisions for them. One issue with mediated settlements, however, is that they are nonbinding in some states. Often, lawyers cleverly protect their own interests by supporting laws that render mediations nonbinding, under the guise that litigants must always have "access to the courts." Nevertheless, unless one or both spouses prove to be compulsively litigious, pure mediation is almost always cheaper, quicker, and more amicable for everyone involved.

When choosing a lawyer, ask them their strategy before you sign any document or pay any retainer. If the first words out of their mouth are not about mediation, don't hire them. You not only want an attorney who is open to the idea of mediation, but you also want one who speaks of it earnestly, even reflexively. You want counsel that speaks of mediation as a first course of action and offers that to the other side. You want to do everything you can to avoid going to court. If your lawyer steers you away from mediation, get rid of them.

Of course, in some cases, mediation cannot work. There are times when couples, burdened by issues that are truly irreconcilable, will contest every point. In such cases, it is best to go directly to court. Although more costly than mediation, going to trial results in binding court orders—albeit orders that one can only hope the court will ultimately enforce.

Attorneys may offer a third option: court-supervised mediation. In this process, the mediator is an actual judge, usually retired, who has the authority to make binding orders. I was advised that this offered the best of mediation along with the best of a trial, as it was both private and binding. However, in my case, it proved to be the opposite. Little was kept private and court orders were violated without comment, let alone penalty. In court-supervised mediation, both sides have the power to fire the mediator, after a specified period, if they are unhappy with specific rulings. Attorneys are vastly skilled at stalling such proceedings until the term of the "rent-a-judge" expires. Court-supervised mediation does have one advantage, however. Unlike a normal civil trial, these records are not open to the public. If you seek privacy in these proceedings for any reason, it keeps many proceedings sealed. If you go to open court, records of divorce proceedings normally become part of the public record and can be accessed by almost anyone. In order to seal documents you have to prove to the court that doing so is in the best interests of the child.

Any system like the family law courts in this country is subject to horrific abuses. The litigants are viewed as pawns who come and go. They suffer through their personal experience and eventually vanish, only to be replaced by another crop of those unfortunate enough to end up in an American divorce court. The guardians of the court system have their game worked out like a major league infield. No one has to tell a ballplayer how to make the double play. He arrives equipped with that instinct. Divorce lawyers and judges arrive at the field equipped with their instincts, as well. No one needs to spell out anything. Everyone is in on the game. As each procedure drifts further away from anything you deem reasonable or fair, let alone in the interests of the child, you have only one source of strength. You just keep repeating "Remember whom you are doing this for."

3

Olives and Cheese

Wꜱᴇɴ ɪ ꜰɪʀꜱᴛ began acting in films, I traveled constantly. I had an apartment on the West Side of Manhattan, but I rarely spent much time there. I would come home from one project, dump my clothes out of my suitcase, repack, and take off again the next day. I regularly flew red-eyes, which meant I had to try to catch some sleep on my rare afternoons at home. My bedroom was at the rear of a building on West Eightieth Street, and behind the building was a school. I would drift off to sleep to the sound of children laughing and squealing in the schoolyard right outside my window.

That sound took me back to my own childhood. When I was growing up, my parents were one of the last generations to have a big family based on hope and faith alone. They had a lot of children and very little money. My dad taught history at a public high school for twenty-eight years and had all kinds of ancillary jobs at the school to supplement his income.

He coached football and riflery along with serving as an academic advisor to student groups after school. All his jobs outside the classroom, however, didn't necessarily take him away from the family. Instead, my dad often let us tag along with him. If you asked me what I was doing, often the answer was whatever my dad was doing.

In the summer, the local schools opened their doors for a recreation program, offering everything from softball leagues to arts and crafts workshops to film screenings. For those three weeks, he wasn't just our dad. He was everyone's dad. His forte was called the "Outdoor Shower." He would pull out a fire hose on hot days and spray down the kids running around the parking lot in bathing suits and sneakers—a little bit of Brooklyn out in the suburbs. When it was over, they served watermelon. Each year, the program ended with a variety show put on by the kids and staff and directed by my father.

On summer weekends my mom and dad would haul my entire family to Jones Beach on Long Island. We'd spend the whole day there. They would cook breakfast and lunch on the beach. We brought with us every piece of athletic equipment imaginable: baseball gloves, volleyball gear, and footballs. At the end of the day we would all pile into the car and head home. On the way, we would stop at the local park, with its enormous swimming pool, to take showers. I once asked my dad why we had to take showers at the park. He replied, "I can't have six kids taking showers all at the same time. It'll back up my septic system." Showers at the public park on the way home: that was my dad.

My childhood was pretty wonderful, all things considered. I always remember what my parents taught me about parenting, not by virtue of their words, but by their actions. They showed me that raising kids isn't about what you can buy or the gifts you give. Being a good parent doesn't mean dropping the child off for the finest music lessons or sending them off to the best camp for the summer. What matters most is the time you spend together. You can give your child many things, but the greatest gifts are your attention and your time.

For me, the greatest thrill in being a parent is witnessing a child developing into his or her own unique self. I used to watch my friends' children and I would try, with little success, to remember what that phase of my own life had been like. You watch them wrestle with all that makes us human, badly at first, then better with each effort. You see them struggle with language and their earliest displays of emotion. Later, I would watch my own daughter's first effort to manipulate me, her first attempt at irony, and telling her first joke. I saw her mother and myself in her, and that delighted me. A greater joy came as she developed in ways apart from either of her parents. Slowly, and then all too quickly, children work to become the people they want to be. My daughter would try this out at the breakfast table when she announced, with all the conviction a seven-year-old can muster, that she was going to be a veterinarian when she grew up. Three weeks later, she wanted to be a dancer, then a singer, then a vet who is also a dancer.

As she grew, we began sharing moments she could not have shared just a couple of months before. Lying on the floor watching television, she would burst out laughing at a beat of humor more sophisticated than what the *Powerpuff Girls* had offered just weeks earlier. While she was watching the show, I was watching her. I watched some of these children's movies thirty times. I knew every line and every gesture in *Snow White* or *Mary Poppins*, and eventually, so did

she. Then the day arrives when your little girl suddenly focuses on how she looks. In one instant, she is a tomboy,
picking up salamanders in the driveway; the next she is
digging through a bag for lip balm and fussing over her
hair. The flurry of these incredible moments goes by like a
single season.

When you lose custody of your child, so much of what is
magical and priceless in this experience is taken away from
you. The moments still occur, but you are no longer there to
share them. You find yourself constantly wondering what
your child is doing now. An overwhelming pain comes from
the knowledge that she is learning life through so many
people's eyes, but least of all your own. You want to share
your own perspective on life, to influence your child, just as
your parents influenced you. Above all, you want to give
your child the gifts of time and attention, but your opportunities become dramatically limited. Often, other men enter
your child's life and fill the void created by your absence.
This isn't necessarily a new man in the mother's life. It
might be the fathers of your child's friends, who spend more
time with your child than you do. In some high-conflict divorces, you can have more conversations with your divorce
lawyer than you have with your child. All the while, the
child experiences life's moments that come only once and
you are not there.

During my marriage, I tried to spend as much time with
my daughter as I could. Like every working parent, my career too often got in the way. Even those who have nine-to-
five jobs miss so much of what happens while they are at the
office. When I wasn't working, I wanted to be with my family and I tried to make the most of our time together. In 1998,

when my daughter was only three, her mother traveled to Africa to make a film in the wake of winning an Oscar earlier that year. I rearranged my schedule and took off from work during that period to spend the entire four months overseas with Ireland. It was during this period that I truly saw that the end of my marriage was coming. As naïve as I was, however, I never once sensed that my relationship with my child would be threatened. There was no feeling of urgency, like when a house burns down and you think of what you can salvage. I never imagined where I would end up. So how might I have planned to stop it?

When my separation began, I was in the middle of directing my first film. The production took place in New York while my daughter was in Los Angeles. Between the shooting schedule and lengthy postproduction, little time was left for commuting to Los Angeles to be a dad. I flew out to L.A. as often as I could to grab a few moments here and there with my daughter. There was never a thought that she would be brought to New York to see me. The situation was far from ideal, but it was all I could do. As soon as the film was completed, I took another project in California so that I could be closer to her. Remarkably, I had no custody orders in that first year. I called and visited at my ex-wife's whim. I took my daughter to lunch or had meals at her home. There was obvious tension between my ex-wife and me. However, it was nothing that seemed to inhibit my visits and certainly nothing that was a precursor of what was to come.

Christmas of 2001 would be my first holiday as a single parent. My ex-wife flew with my daughter to upstate New York to drop her off at my sister's house. We stayed in a hotel that first night, and as I was leaving, my daughter asked where I was going. I told her I was going to my sister's and she would spend the night at the hotel with her mom. Unless, I suggested, she wanted to come and begin her visit with us that evening. Like a shot, my daughter said she wanted to come with me. I will never forget that moment. My sister and I looked quickly and saw that my ex-wife, normally a rather inscrutable individual, looked as if she had been hit by an electric current. She quickly gathered herself and said, "Well... then... you go on and stay with them, and I will call you tomorrow." As we walked to the car, my sister commented, "I don't think she's going to bring her up here again."

After that holiday, things began to change rapidly, and I faced what many noncustodial parents experience. A fence suddenly goes up around your child. The custodial parent, along with lawyers, judges, and court-ordered therapists, are the gatekeepers. Decisions regarding when you can see your child and how much time you will have with her are no longer yours to make. You may request time, you may beg, but others now have the final say. The court intervenes and solicits the opinions and insights of "experts." Your former spouse and his or her lawyers begin to make their formal case in a family law courtroom. As a friend once told me, "They will paint a picture of you on your worst day and say that is who you are. They will pathologize your most casual utterances and criminalize most of your daily behavior." I was about to slam up against of the worst of it.

In high-conflict divorce cases, the idea of parenting itself is transformed. It suddenly ceases to be about giving your child your time and attention. Rather, it becomes one more filing, declaration, or deposition. Even in those enviable situations where divorced couples work together to effectively co-parent their children, the distance divorce creates makes being a parent more difficult. That is why so many noncustodial parents find it necessary to walk away. Walking away was never an option for me early on, however, as something happened to me around Christmas of 2001 while at my sister's house. I met one of my sister's friends, a man I will call Tom. Tom was divorced, and as we spoke, his words were to become like a curse put on me. Tom told me, "I did everything my ex-wife asked me to do in the early months and years. She told me to stay away and give her and my daughters their space. It proved to be a disaster and a mistake. Don't do it, Alec. Always remember, if you don't fight for your daughter, she will never forgive you when she gets older."

AS I SAT in a London hotel room, six months later, my attorney informed me that my ex-wife's divorce petition had arrived at her office. She wanted to know if I wanted to see it right away. "It's pretty rough," she said. "Maybe you should read it when you finish shooting." I told her to send it over to me. A couple of days later, I sat and read the document. It was one of the saddest days of my life, up until that time. Filled with more revisionistic and unkind language than I could have ever imagined, it was the first of a series of such blows I would encounter. Now the phones were all cut off and I could not call my five-year-old daughter. She began to become a collection of photos on my walls. The moats were dug. It was June of 2002 and we were just getting started.

EARLY ON, I DID NOT have a home in Los Angeles and would stay in hotels when I flew out. The gatekeepers declared that children need a proper home to go to for overnight visits with a parent. In their opinion hotels do not provide a suitable, child-friendly environment. Therefore, I rented a house in the area. Then my ex declared that my house was too far away from the child's primary residence. I moved closer, but gained nothing. No matter how much I attempted to accommodate my ex, the court simultaneously made rulings that limited my time with my child based upon my ex-wife's characterizations of me as a father. The net result of my ex-wife's declarations was like being thrown into a deep pit. Sadly for the alienated parent, the judges and attorneys involved know that many men are going to attempt to claw their way out of that pit, no matter what the cost is physically or emotionally. Your relationship with your child is literally at stake. The only question is whether you will run out of money before you make it.

During the long and tortured process during which some judge is deciding if you truly are the unfit parent that your ex is contending, precious time is rushing by. For more than a year, I had to content myself with six hours on Saturday afternoons in a park or toy store with my little girl, or a ninety-minute dinner in the middle of the week. My first overnight visit with her did not come until Christmas of 2001, a full year after my separation date. Even then, I was ordered to bring my ex-wife's nanny with me.

After my daughter started first grade, I volunteered to come in once or twice a week to read to the children at her school. Schools ordinarily welcome parental involvement, even from noncustodial parents. Some children, however, are not always as eager to have their parents hanging around the school. Therefore, I asked my daughter on more than one occasion if it was all right with her that I continue volunteering. I told her I did not want to embarrass her or make her feel uncomfortable. At the time I was one of very few fathers who volunteered for this program. But my daughter would always cut me short and tell me that she wanted me there. She would also ask me to stay and eat lunch with her.

The challenge noncustodial parents face is to try to create normalcy when nothing is normal. Parenting is something that happens in the regular flow of life, but when you lose custody of your child, you are cut off from that flow. You are viewed as actually interrupting that flow, which has now been established by the custodial parent and the court. Your new house, which you bring your child to, is unfamiliar. Everything the two of you do is tightly scheduled. You begin to look at clocks and calendars with a slight desperation. You find yourself fighting the sensation that you are somehow competing with the other parent for your child's affection. Some parents overcompensate by indulging their child's every whim. Others find themselves so exhausted from the combined strain of legal wrangling and career that they have little left to offer their child when they do have time together. More than anything, you long to establish a place where you both can truly feel at home, even if only for a weekend.

Eventually I was able to establish a more regular visitation schedule with my daughter that included overnight visits. I rented a house where, in spite of the spasms of disruptive litigation, she would spend every other weekend with me. Although I lived in the house only when I was in Los Angeles for that visitation, I tried to fill it with the things I knew she liked. Just as I did when I was married, I would light a fire and put on one of her favorite movies. One cloudy afternoon she had settled down on the couch and I asked her if she wanted a snack. Looking up at me, sleepily, she asked me if I had any olives and cheese. I had seen this coming, so you can bet that my pantry was filled with jars of olives and I had a block of cheese in the refrigerator the size of the Manhattan phone directory. "Yes," I told her, "would you like some?" She smiled up at me and said, "Yes, please." As I walked out of the room I glanced back at my daughter lying there, content. I was overwhelmed and began to sob, hiding from her in the kitchen. "What are you doing?" she demanded. "Come watch the movie with me." I told her I was cleaning the kitchen and would be right there.

I could not help but wonder about how many moments like this I had missed. All I wanted to do was make my daughter happy, and for now, she was. I pulled myself together and walked back into the room to ask her if she needed anything else. All she wanted was for me to sit down and join her. I realized that this is all I wanted, too. I was suddenly overcome with the thought that no one could come through the door and take this from me. In this moment, I realized that this rented house held nothing familiar for either of us except each other. It was not her house and it was not mine either, but that did not matter now. My daughter and I, on that afternoon, had made a home.

4

Are You Done Yet?

Dennis Wasser is a lean, well-dressed man with a thatch of carefully coiffed, silver hair. He bears a resemblance to deposed California governor Gray Davis. Wasser is a major player in the Los Angeles divorce community and will tell you so. Wasser is a big fan of Wasser, and after fifteen minutes in his presence, I expected to find a full-length oil painting of him in his office. Wasser was the polar opposite of Bob Kaufman, my previous attorney. Where Kaufman was feral and intense, Wasser was sedate and detached. He was well versed in handling high-profile divorces, he assured me. Kirk Kerkorian, Tom Cruise, and many other Hollywood celebrities and elite had turned to him as they went through the same difficult time in their lives. He told me that these powerful people trusted him and so should I. The message lawyers like Wasser send is to leave everything to them. Don't focus on the cost. They will take care of everything.

As it turned out, I was not Wasser material. I peppered him with questions about how and why the family law system works as it does. I was trying to do the one thing many attorneys find most annoying: to better understand the process in order to manage the cost of my divorce. The Wasser team included Susan Carter, an arid woman who largely concentrated on the financial settlement issues of a divorce. She found my questions particularly tedious. During our few sessions together I would ask her why certain steps had to be taken. I asked how California family law had evolved and thus prohibited fairer and more effective ways of handling the issues we were reviewing. I asked why judges would allow certain conflicting actions or statements to go unchallenged and how a system so blatantly inefficient, if not corrupt, could be tolerated by the members of her profession. Carter's physical reaction made it clear that I was there to answer, not ask, her questions. On other occasions my curiosity was met with nothing but a blank stare, as if I were not even in the room. Later, I learned she was going through a divorce of her own.

In the beginning Wasser tolerated me. "Alec, Alec," he would say, "very important people with lives at least as complicated as yours trust me to take care of these things for them." Why, he wondered, was I resisting him? With time the geniality faded. He came to regard my attempts to keep the costs down with disdain, bordering on vulgarity. Dennis Wasser catered to wealthy, privileged people, offering only the finest professional counseling to his clients. If you had to ask how much this would cost, you obviously could not afford his services. I quickly sensed that my net worth did not compare to many of Wasser's other clients. Even if it did, I considered throwing money into the pit of the family law system to be an unconscionable waste, a conviction I did not hesitate to share with my attorneys.

The financial settlement is typically the first area to be decided in a divorce case, as money must necessarily start flowing in some direction, especially where children are involved. In my own case, however, I found this odd, since the division of property and support payments proved less important than custody decisions, as little was in serious dispute regarding support issues in my case. Custody-related issues seemed far more urgent. When you are the noncustodial parent, time works against you. If your former spouse is not open and cooperative regarding divorced co-parenting, every day you spend disconnected from your child is another day in which that child adjusts to life without you. Although you may call regularly, or visit on alternating weekends, your influence in a child's day-to-day life wanes. It is as though the child takes her love for you and places it on a shelf. The longer it takes for you to get a set of meaningful custody orders, the more distance time creates between the two of you, and the longer it will take for you to resuscitate that relationship. Even though financial settlements are fairly formulaic, settling them takes time. When the settlement conference has to accommodate not only your schedule and that of your former spouse, but also the schedules of two sets of attorneys, forensic accountants, a judge or family law commissioner, and everyone else involved in the process, time stretches into months, if not years. In my own case, more than a year and a half went by between the date that a mediator was hired and the financial settlement agreements were reached. Only then did we move decisively on to the custody evaluation phase of the case.

Retired Judge Jill Robbins was hired in the late fall of 2001 as the family law commissioner, or "rent-a-judge," who would hear our case in mediation. She was a brash, colorful woman who reminded me of Joy Behar from *The View.* Robbins already had established relationships with the attorneys on both sides of the case, having retired as a California family law judge a few years earlier. Most, if not all, of the private family law commissioners in California are retired family law judges. When you walk into these rooms as a litigant, you are the outsider. Each of the other parties is already well acquainted with the others. Prior to dropping the gavel to commence her proceedings, Robbins and the other attorneys would share anecdotes about their families or their latest vacations.

Such familiarity does not work in your favor. Private judges in such cases are selected by both sets of attorneys. Therefore, judges, both private rent-a-judges acting as family law commissioners as well as judges in open court, rarely admonish, reprimand, or sanction attorneys nor make harsh rulings against them. Such actions would keep these judges from being invited back to the party. A lawyer must make an egregious procedural error to be rebuked by a judge. Instead, all the familiar parties work quite hard to keep one another from looking bad. Like nearly all such systems, the attitude is that the clients come and go, but the principal players remain the same. These players need to maintain healthy working relationships with one another in order to keep the machinery of the system, which they are enriched by, churning along. Today it is your turn to have decisions made that will affect you and your children for the rest of your lives. Tomorrow someone else will be sitting across the table. The names and faces of the litigants may change, but the game remains the same.

THE FINANCIAL SETTLEMENT PHASE of the proceedings involved a lot of discovery and filings, followed by a few day-long sessions of argument before Robbins. After that, we moved through a handful of supplemental proceedings that dealt with items as silly as the location of an antique blanket. Logic often goes out the window and judges may refuse to impose any reason or restraint on the attorneys and their distorted representations of their clients' money issues. Many divorce attorneys who handle cases for women, regardless of the assets of the family, tend to operate within a basic framework. Gary, an art dealer, is fifty years old. He lives in New York and has two children. Gary's story regarding his financial settlement phase is both typical and instructive.

> GARY: Prior to our marriage, my wife's books sold well and she made a good living. When we discussed getting married after living together for a couple of years, I asked if she wanted me to sign a prenup. She had married and divorced her first husband without one. He had prevailed in court, and she was ordered to pay him a substantial sum of money over a period of several years. She had sounded bitter about all of it and it was with that in mind that I asked if she wanted to handle our situation differently. She said no, unequivocally. She said, "What's yours is yours and what's mine is mine and if we divorce, we'll just shake hands and walk away."
>
> Later, during our first settlement conference, her lawyer asked for more than $100,000 per month and wanted me to pay for her office-related expenses, as

well. After the lawyers argued for several months, she ultimately received less than 20 percent of that.

In spite of whatever unreasonable demands were made in my own case, Judge Robbins did not dismiss those requests out of hand. After one full day of negotiation, I began to understand how that part of the game was played. The "petitioner" makes their case, asking for whatever amount of money they maintain that they require, employing a combination of genuine need and/or malice and/or their attorney's avarice. Both sets of lawyers know this course and how the greens break. They know that the more ridiculous the demands, the more contentious the process becomes. Thus, the greater the legal fees that are generated. It is a self-perpetuating system.

I believed that my lawyers were usually pretty straight with me throughout this process. They suggested actions that would allow me to circumvent some of the more unnecessary battles. Early on they discerned that the other side would rarely, if ever, suggest anything constructive. Thus, my attorneys knew that a more expeditious end to these proceedings would have to come from our side.

During the formal proceedings, Wasser was the front man, and like all good front men, he was prepared for whatever might happen from the moment he stepped onstage. The other attorneys on the team prepared the documentation and briefs, but it was Wasser who did the talking, and he did not disappoint. Unlike my ex-wife's counsel, Wasser was intelligent, aggressive, and calm, all in the same instant. Of all of the people I encountered, he was the most talented and compelling. Watching him perform, I felt sorry for him

that he had squandered such talent in the sewer of Los Angeles family law.

Dennis Wasser made short work of the preliminary financial demands of the other side. With just the right amount of
indignation and with impeccable timing, he quickly moved
through the items on their list. By the time he was done, he
had raised doubts about nearly 75 percent of the other side's
original demands. Judge Robbins seemed to enjoy Wasser.
To watch a skilled lawyer school someone like Neal Hersh,
my ex's lawyer, was something to see. Yet I found myself
wondering if all of this was simply a game these attorneys
played. The other side made some outlandish demand. Wasser
then stepped in and did his thing. In the end, we arrived
right where we should have had we been in a real mediation.
Was I played by these people? How many times had these attorneys and this judge made these very same moves? Is this
how all divorce proceedings unfold, every move tacitly cho-
reographed to appear spontaneous and equitable? Wasser
saved me a lot of money that day, or so it appeared. Eventually, however, much of that would go to his firm in legal fees.

At one point in the midst of the financial settlement phase
of my case, Dennis Wasser came into a conference room with
a strange look on his face. "Are you done yet?" he asked. I
begged his pardon, and he repeated his question. "I see you
and your wife in the room together and I can't be sure if
you're really done yet. I've watched a lot of couples go
through this process and I wonder if your marriage is really
over." I was completely stunned. Was he simply being polite? Provocative? What did he see in the past day or two
that led him to believe the two of us had any hope? Or, more
likely, was this just some kind of psychological test? His

question smacked of a no-turning-back moment, as if to say that the proceedings could potentially become truly ugly and any hopes of reconciliation would soon be squashed forever. I managed a nervous laugh and assured Dennis that I knew Kim, and once she was done with you, she was done. Within weeks, the financial settlement was over. In those negotiations, we had sent signals of real conciliation to their side. There were provisions in the agreement that I thought would earn me some real psychic equity with my ex for our future proceedings. But nothing would be further from the truth.

IN THIS PHASE, the lawyers of both parties can do a lot of damage by exploiting the financial insecurities of the other side, particularly those of mothers with children.

> GARY: My lawyer taught me early on that my wife's lawyer was known in the divorce community as the "hand-holder" of the female litigant. Her attorney basically told her that men my age and in my income range would likely remarry and start another family. He warned her that the time to protect her own economic future and that of her children was "right now, in this room." He told her that they needed to get tough, get me in a headlock, and get as much money as they could, even if they used the children as leverage. He told her that she wasn't doing this for herself, but for the children. She, in turn, repeated to me, "I'm not doing this for me. This money isn't for me. I'm doing this to protect my children." Then she asked for five times the amount I was eventually ordered to pay.

Of course, financial settlement conferences are necessary, and often the difficulties that arise are the result of individuals who attempt to hide assets. *Forbes* magazine estimates that in as many as one-half of all divorces nationwide, one spouse or the other hides assets, with few negative repercussions.[1] Men and women who seek to conceal their true assets or distort that picture in any way make life difficult for others. Susan, forty-five, a stockbroker in Northern California, experienced this firsthand.

> SUSAN: My husband quit his job as our marriage entered its final period. He said that he wanted more time with the children and that he would continue to do consulting. But I think he spoke with an attorney or perhaps a friend. Someone told him that the court would likely average our last three years of income. I later found out he was paid a lot of money in cash by certain clients, in order to crash his reported income. He had been receiving cash payments for several months before we separated.

Among the more disconcerting things that I felt during the financial settlement phase of my own case was the sense of invasion of privacy. You come into court and you are required not only to empty all of your pockets, but also to submit to a strip search, as well. Forensic accountants will add to your bill by going over every receipt, contract, and slip of paper you have ever known. Even you do not know what you are actually worth until forensic accountants show you. Nothing tells others more about you than what you spend your money on, or do not spend it on, for that matter. Even though you assume that the legal professionals in the room

---

[1] Richard C. Morais, "Divorce Dirty Tricks," *Forbes*, vol. 178, no. 10, November 13, 2006, p. 174.

have seen and heard it all, you cannot help but feel a vague sense of embarrassment. Add to this that the lawyers on both sides now know, inarguably, how much money you have and, therefore, how deep into this hole you can go. And they do not hesitate to throw you down as deep as they possibly can. David, a writer living in Boston, aged sixty, recalls how his experience is far from the exception:

DAVID: The judge had a pile of papers in front of him, all of my financials. At the bottom of one page was a total of all the cash I had accrued. All the money I had, literally. The judge tapped the figure on the sheet and said, "Give her this and I will recommend that they accept and settle." My lawyer knew it was 30 percent more than we had calculated she deserved, even on the high end. But my lawyer believed, even at this early stage, that the judge sensed that my wife would make it difficult over every issue. Her lawyer had her right where he wanted her. My own attorney concurred and said, "You're an earner. Money you can get. You're buying peace of mind." I gave her the money. I gave a lot in the financial settlement, including a big piece of my retirement savings. I settled in order to facilitate a better relationship with my ex. She barely looked at me throughout and, when we were done, said nothing. From what I read in the papers, I ended up paying more in actual child support than Donald Trump or Ron Perlman. Everyone there knew she was a high-maintenance woman, and everyone shrugged it off, as if to say this is what happens when you marry a woman like this and it goes wrong.

A prenuptial agreement might have avoided some of David's problems. Unfortunately, he did not have one. A prenuptial agreement is, potentially, the single greatest remedy against prolonged, bitter divorce battles. Some reject prenups as a vulgar, unromantic foreshadowing cast before a marriage begins. However, it is, in fact, an insurance policy that protects both parties. At a time when half of all marriages end in divorce, wisdom demands that such an agreement be executed while both parties actually have a shred of respect for each other. I recall that every individual that I spoke with about their contentious divorce proceedings who did not have a prenup wished that they had drafted one. I did not have a prenup when I got married. In spite of my eyewitness observations of my ex's demeanor and decision-making process during her 1993 trial, I trusted that she would never wish to put anyone, particularly herself, through an experience even remotely like that. I rolled the dice and trusted that if our marriage came to an end, lawyers would not be necessary.

There are aspects of divorce litigation that cannot be pre-empted or controlled by a prenuptial agreement. Laws have been passed in many states (conveniently for lawyers and therapists) that ultimately render some premarital agreements unenforceable, especially involving child custody. As is so often the case in family law courtrooms, nearly any aspect of a prenup can be disallowed or reversed if a litigant has enough money and a lawyer with a firm grasp of the code. It is safe to assume, however, that some provisions of prenups may stand up in court or at least clearly state the will of the parties at the time they were married.

ONCE A FINANCIAL SETTLEMENT agreement is reached, the proceedings move to the selection of the custody evaluator.

The evaluator is a therapist appointed by the court to render a recommendation to the judge regarding the permanent custody orders for the child or children. Wasser passed me on to his in-house custody attorney, Vicki Greene. In a session with Wasser and Greene, and later with the opposing counsel, the lawyers bandied about the names of custody evaluators whom they each proposed for my case. This would prove to be one of the most pivotal decisions in the proceedings. They talked repeatedly about how one evaluator had treated their client in a particular case, or how they distrusted another from a different case. The lawyers stated outright that a particular therapist is fair or is "pro-fathers," but eventually I learned the truth about the relationship between law firms and evaluators. Law firms hire evaluators. The two firms get together and they propose a list of those they will approve. The judge must sanction that choice, but the law firms are essentially left alone to work out their own arrangement. Evaluators who operate inside the family law system are dependent on the law firms for their livelihood. The court does not choose the therapist, although it may under certain circumstances. Because the law firms typically make these choices, because there is no blind hiring, there is a perceived conflict of interest. You enter the evaluator's office and that therapist is beholden to both law firms. Not beholden to either of the clients, not to any of the children involved in the case, not even to the truth. Clients come and go but, under this system, the evaluators and the law firms are forever. The therapists are indebted to the lawyers, and that is a debt that the therapists never forget.

5

In the Best Interests of the Child

I DO NOT THINK I have ever been as anxious and filled with fear in my life as I was before, during, and after my custody evaluation, which began in 2002. At this point, the custody phase of my litigation had been passed on to Vicki Greene, who was Wasser's custody specialist. Vicki is married with two children. Trim and always dressed in conservative business attire, Vicki is an attractive woman, in spite of her thick glasses. She no doubt earned those glasses from years of reading copious documents and briefs. Vicki's eyes, it seemed, were nearly always red.

After months of dealing with judges, my own attorneys, and opposing counsel, Vicki was like a tank of oxygen. I felt like I was living the scene from *Rosemary's Baby*, where Mia Farrow exults in finding Dr. Hill, the Charles Grodin character, later to discover that he is also a part of the conspiracy. Vicki, thankfully, was genuine. Others I had worked with were equally capable and carried impeccable credentials, but Vicki seemed like a real person. She had normal reactions of empathy toward me and the painful realities of parental alienation that were enveloping my case. Others were impatient with my questions, but Vicki acknowledged how inefficient and unfair the system was. She genuinely wanted to help find a solution to my dilemma. Vicki, I sensed, had come to truly care about me and, more important, about my relationship with my daughter. However, Vicki's sensitivity and humanity may have ultimately caused nearly as many problems as they solved.

I BELIEVE THAT THE DEFAULT position of every family court in this country should be fifty-fifty physical custody of the couple's children. The only exceptions should be those commonly held objections that include spousal and/or child abuse, drug and/or alcohol abuse by a potential custodial parent, or a parent's inability to provide a home for children for any number of economic or emotional reasons. Any parent should be treated with an assumption of innocence when it comes to whatever "charges" they are facing from their ex-spouse and their attorneys. However, this is not the case in American family law. A parent, and more commonly a mother, can reduce or outright eliminate another parent's custody/visitation rights with little more than innuendo, unsubstantiated charges, or the assertions of clearly compromised and biased witnesses. Courts will set aside the parental rights of the "accused" until the completion of the custody evaluation, conducted by a therapist selected by lawyers, but commissioned by the judge. That evaluation can take months or, in some cases, years.

Custody evaluators are charged with the job of helping

the court to determine what custody and/or visitation arrangements are in the child's best interest. I grew to believe, however, that evaluations such as these are also mechanisms by which judges and lawyers deflect their responsibility and pass it on to the therapeutic community. No judge wants to hand over custody to the wrong person. Judges, therefore, often share much of their decision making with evaluators. Although judges are technically not bound by an evaluator's recommendations, a long-form, primary custody evaluation can function like a Magna Carta throughout your case. It is one document that attorneys will reference over and over again, depending on which client, if any, is favored in the report. At times, attorneys fall back on it as if it holds an almost Talmudic level of wisdom.

You go to a therapist's office and you answer questions. No one from your lawyer's office goes with you to brief you on your rights. No one is there to coach you on what to say or to offer you any advice on how to best obtain the results you are after. Once I entered into my evaluation, I was alone in a room with a person who would wield tremendous power over my life and my right to access the person who is most precious to me. Divorce litigation is the civil proceeding that metes out criminal punishments, insofar as it takes away your truly God-given rights. That process begins with the evaluation. A woman I will call Marcia Rydell was the evaluator in my case, and the moment I laid eyes on her, I was worried.

I sat in the waiting room, on time, of course. I pressed the button that triggers the light inside to alert the therapist that I was there. Marcia Rydell opened the door. A remarkably pale, almost cadaverous woman, Rydell looked like something out of an Edward Gorey illustration. I sat on a sofa in her office, and she asked some preliminary questions. (Where to send the bill?) She made brief comments about what her procedures were and spoke in a rather timid and remarkably quiet voice. One could say that if I had set out to read this woman and tailor my presentation to her personality, I would have spoken very slowly, unemotionally, and in hushed tones. However, I did not do that.

I sat across from Rydell, her demeanor totally impassive and registering nothing. I told her what I believed to be the truth. I told Rydell that my ex-wife was a woman whom I once loved deeply, in spite of the fact that we were largely incompatible. I told her that my ex-wife was someone who had struggled to maintain ongoing intimate relationships. I stated that she had few friends in her life who were not on her payroll and who, therefore, rarely crossed the line into the level of honesty and openness that constitutes real friendship. I told Rydell that this is common at the highest levels of the entertainment business. I told her that my ex-wife was mercurial and prone to wide swings in her feelings for others. I told her that my ex-wife had been married for seven years to another man, and once she had divorced him, as far as I know, she never spoke to him again. I told her that my ex-wife was an individual who basically lived by one rule: once she was done with you, she was done with you. After that, a friendship, or any kind of working relationship, was out of the question.

On an emotional level, these sessions got to be extremely anguished rather quickly. To sit there and tell this complete stranger the facts and my interpretations of them in the hope that she would appreciate who I was and all I had been through simply overwhelmed me. Within a matter of minutes, I was sobbing in Rydell's office and telling her some of the more intimate details of how my marriage withered and died. *There is so much riding on this*, I thought. I wanted this woman, whom I could not read at all, to understand, at the very least, that I loved my daughter with every molecule of my body. That all I wanted was to have an important role in her life. I wanted to show my child the world through my eyes and, in turn, let her show me the world through hers. I wanted Rydell to realize that to base her evaluation of me or my situation on any statements made by my ex-wife or any of her paid associates was unfair. I wanted the state-sanctioned, court-ordered custody evaluator to understand that I was a victim of parental alienation. Rydell said nothing. I had come to this initial meeting primed for some cathartic episode, and this is what I got.

Rydell looked at me at one point, during one of the earlier sessions, and asked, "How do I know you aren't acting?" My train of thought stopped dead in its tracks. "I beg your pardon?" I asked. She wondered aloud how much she could rely upon the assertions and testimony of a professional performer. "You're a pretty good actor," she said. "How do I know whether to believe you?" I took this in for a moment and said, "Do you think if I was acting I would be as forceful and honest with you about all of this? Don't you think I would have come in here and been more manipulative, played it so much more in control? You want to see acting, wait until she gets here," I said, referring to my ex-wife. Rydell just sat there, silently. Rydell's unusual question represented a critical moment in my understanding of the process and of evaluators like her. In a state of near panic, I began to realize, after two or three sessions, that telling the truth in her office was a potential mistake. Rydell was a part of the system. It appeared that she wanted to keep the court-ordered litigants flowing into her office. For her to accomplish that, she could not actually do all or most of what would be required in order to truly understand what I had been dealing with.

The thought of manipulating Rydell in any way, either directly or by coaching the testimony of others, never occurred to me. Perhaps it should have. With no coaching or advice from my own attorneys, I was left to figure out for myself what was in the best interest of my relationship with my daughter. Rydell's own demeanor, her utter lack of a discernible reaction to anything I said, let alone any curiosity about me or about my true parenting history, created a vacuum. Initially, I had decided to fill that vacuum. I sensed that if any ultimate decisions by the judge were based on Rydell's actual level of interest in my assertions, the evaluation would have been incomplete and over with rather quickly. Therefore, I tried desperately to convince Rydell to care about what I was going through, but to no avail.

I began to sense that she had already made up her mind about me and about my ex-wife. She seemed, like so many professionals who make their living in family law, unwilling to do the heavy lifting required to root out the truth of my situation. There just wasn't enough time. There were other litigants. The light on the wall switched on, indicating that one was already outside in the waiting room. Because there wasn't time to understand what was really going on in my life, Marcia Rydell was going to make this a

little easier on herself. Every time I spoke of parental alienation, Rydell changed the subject. It was as if I had brought
up the grassy knoll in Dallas or Area 51 in Nevada. In professional terms, it was against her religion. Therefore, it was
not worthy of our time. I pressed on, driven by a need to
make my case. My life with my child could be at stake. Rydell never flinched.

Meanwhile, during the earliest stages of my separation,
my visitation was something I simply worked out with my
ex-wife. I would call, come over with lunch, or take my
daughter to dinner or shopping or the movies. Although
there was never any discussion of overnight visitation, I saw
my daughter with some regularity. Neither party had filed
formal declarations yet, so a court-ordered visitation schedule did not exist. While visiting my daughter, there were
obvious tensions between my ex and me, but everything
seemed to function fairly well. There were no arguments or
scenes played out, in front of the child or otherwise. I had a
reflexive, yet very real, desire to reconcile with my wife. It
was in that spirit that I did not challenge Kim when she
would either grant or withhold time with my daughter in a
completely arbitrary way. Early on, I sensed that Kim
wanted me to see my daughter at my ex-wife's whim. There
was never any discussion with her, not once, about my
rights, responsibilities, or the importance of my contribu-
tion as a parent. Very quickly, my daughter had one parent,
as far as I understood a parent's role in the life of a child. I
was relegated to a role that was more akin to an uncle or
even less than that.

One day, early in the process, I was sitting in a car with
my daughter, who was then five. We were on our way to the

movies. This was one of the first times that my daughter seemed overtly thoughtful and uncomfortable about the situation. I asked her if she was all right. She nodded, stiffly. Then she said, "Mommy says we can all be together again if you go and get help. Mommy says you're sick." At a later visit with Rydell, I told her that I thought it was inappropriate, to say the least, for the child's mother to be making such statements. Rydell neither registered nor said anything. I realized that, although I was wrong to expect Rydell to carry messages back and forth between the two parties and to function as an ersatz mediator, Rydell had no intention of investigating my complaint. I realized that those things that I believed were detrimental to my relationship with my daughter (and are also considered so by any number of experts outside of Rydell's office) would get no airing here. Rydell did not particularly care what Kim said to Ireland about me. Eventually, I relayed more such stories to her. She didn't seem to care about them either. Unfortunately, my experience is not unique. As Gary's statement will attest, some evaluators overlook issues that one is certain would be and should be determinative in child custody.

> GARY: My wife, Lynn, drank quite a bit during our marriage. It didn't occur to me that she had a problem when we first got together. We met at my gallery, where she had come to an event with her friend. In the months that followed, she appeared to always have a glass of wine in her hand, but I didn't really notice because she was always so happy, so content. Her books were selling well. Her career was in a wonderful place. Soon after we were living together, her sales started to

fall. She had a couple of unsuccessful books in a row, and she started to get depressed and bitter. Her drinking increased a bit. Then her editor retired and passed Lynn on to someone Lynn didn't like. By then we were married and things went down from there and quickly. Lynn was dropped by her publisher and soon she drank every night. She sat at home in the kitchen, either slightly buzzed or seriously smashed, watching television. She would saunter off to bed and collapse at around nine thirty. I did not drink at all, having chosen to get sober several years earlier. When I met Lynn, so many things about her led me to believe that she was ripe for sobriety. I never thought her drinking was a real problem until we were already married. She quit completely during both pregnancies, but after our children came, she only drank more in response to the pressure. During our custody evaluation, I told the evaluator that Lynn was an alcoholic. My attorney said that any charges of alcohol or drug abuse would trigger a mandatory alcohol and drug abuse evaluation. The evaluator never performed that evaluation. Eventually she said she didn't have time, as both sets of attorneys seemed to be in such a hurry for her to finish her report. I had submitted the declarations of several collateral witnesses who knew that Lynn had a drinking problem. The evaluator simply ignored them.

I provided a list of "collateral witnesses" to Rydell during my evaluation, as well. These were individuals who would, presumably, substantiate many of my statements. Nearly all of those people were friends of mine who, as I understood it, would be called upon to testify as to what they had witnessed during my marriage and, in particular, how I functioned as a father. Collateral witnesses ought to play a vital role in such evaluations. Once an evaluator has discerned what constitutes a reliable collateral witness, the testimony of such reliable witnesses should figure rather heavily in their report.

There are family members, employees, and certain friends who serve only to corroborate a particular litigant's story. Your list is yours to make. In my own case, it should have been clear, from the most cursory examination, that neither my family nor my ex-wife's family was truly impartial. My own list—and I attempted to highlight this to Rydell— was comprised of people who relied on me for nothing, people who derived no economic benefit from our relationship. They were people who had spent volumes of time with my daughter and me together and had seen that she was, at the very least, as happy, safe, and engaged in her relationship with me as she was with her mother. Many of the people on Kim's list were her employees, people for whom honest appraisals of me as a father might cost them their jobs.

Custody evaluations quickly become another contest of wills between the litigants and their attorneys. The evaluators have little time, or so it seems, to actually vet much of the information and emotionally charged assertions that are presented to them. Evaluators must sift through the recollections of bitter husbands and wives, their friends, colleagues, and families, as they all strain to offer their side. One would think that the modus operandi of some of these "witnesses" would be clear to a therapist who observes people for a living. However, in the realm of custody evaluation, your best and most honest witnesses may be ignored, while some of the most obviously compromised ones have the greatest impact.

GARY: Within days after my ex had filed her official divorce papers, Vera, one of the housekeepers who worked for my ex, called me to say she had been terminated. I had always enjoyed a very pleasant relationship with the staff of the house and with Vera in particular. Vera told me that all of the staff was gathered into the kitchen one day recently and Patty, Lynn's lawyer, informed each person that they were to sign statements against me or they would lose their jobs. They were provided with outlines of what to say and were to sign sworn statements that they had overheard me screaming at and otherwise verbally abusing my ex-wife repeatedly during the term of their employ. Every member signed the statements against me, except Vera. Over the telephone, Vera told me that the other women on the staff did not want to sign the documents against me, either. "We all knew you were a good father," she said, "but we were told we had to either sign the papers or lose our jobs." (I had wondered if some of these women were actually illegal aliens, although they had presented what I presumed to be valid documentation.) When I asked Vera why she refused to sign she said that if they would do this to her, she worried about what else they were capable of.

My wife told the evaluator, as well as the judge and anyone else who would listen, that I screamed and yelled a lot, too. I think that if I did it to the extent that she insisted, our relationship would not have lasted one weekend, let alone ten years. Like all couples in a contentious divorce, my ex sought to paint a picture of me on my worst day and tell the world that this is who I really was. During my life, I have lost my temper and pretty badly. I acknowledge that and, as you will discover later, worked pretty hard to remedy that.

There were certain aspects of my wife's own behavior that I found alternately alarming, inappropriate, off-putting, or rude, but I never imagined I might use them to diminish her custody of her child. In the divorce process, male behavior is pathologized in a way that similar behavior by a woman is not. If a male astronaut drives hundreds of miles in a car packed with an array of items used to abduct someone, bound for a location where he will confront his romantic rival, all the while wearing adult diapers in order to hasten the journey, that man is deeply disturbed and dangerous and must be confined. The female astronaut who does this is portrayed as "heartsick."

GARY: I was having a rather heated discussion one day, all worked up with my assistant and instructing her on what to say to someone who had reneged on a deal we had. I was in another room, and when I came out, my daughter said, "Mommy says you yell all the time and that's bad." I asked my daughter if I yelled all of the time when I was around her. She chuckled and said, "No! My mom yells ten times more than you do." There was a pause and then she added, "But when you do it, it's different."

My ex-wife made some pretty harsh assertions about me as the process got rolling in the spring of 2002. The informal arrangement that we had had during the previous few months dissolved. In mediation with Judge Robbins, I acknowledged that the schedule for a film I was producing and directing required I remain in New York for nearly eight months in 2001. In bargaining for a piece of that summer with my daughter, I agreed to a visitation schedule that was offensive, to say the least. I would see my daughter from 12 P.M. to 6 P.M. on Saturday and Sunday every other weekend, and have a weekday dinner for ninety minutes. The total amount of time I would see her would be twenty-seven hours a month. I was desperate to lock in the time with my daughter for that summer, so I agreed. It was here that I discovered my ex's attorney's greatest gift, which was to make motions, or threaten them, in order to corner his opposition so that you bargain away something you might later win at a lengthy trial. He runs out the clock. Summer happens on schedule; the court cannot delay it. If you want summer visitation, you bargain away something else now to get it. If you choose to fight and hold formal hearings (always an option in state-sponsored mediation), the calendar may work against you. Robbins, on more than one occasion, would instruct me that the other side had run out the clock. Therefore, I would likely have had no choice but to accede to their demands in order to protect my summer visitation.

March of 2002 arrived, and Kim wanted to change the arrangements regarding my telephone contact, as well. Her answer was to disconnect all of her phone lines, without warning, and force me to go to Robbins in order to litigate the phone issue. By this time, I was getting desperate. On one occasion, I took my daughter and her friend to the movies. The other girl's mother, whom I knew somewhat from my daughter's school, was supposed to come along. When I arrived at the theater, the mother was there with not only her other children, but also her own mother and her brother. I was silently enraged. This episode became an issue in subsequent hearings, as it is wrong for any parent in divorce to schedule the other parent's time. These people were perfectly nice and I would go on to spend some pleasant afternoons with them down the road. However, I had so little time with my daughter as it was. I was heading to London soon and wanted complete control over how to schedule my precious time with my daughter.

I TOLD ALL of this to Rydell. She was unmoved. In the past several weeks, what had seemed like an imperfect yet working dynamic between my ex and me had quickly become thermonuclear. The phones were cut off. My ex had no respect for any boundaries regarding my relationship with my child. My own collateral witnesses had discredited much of what Kim and her witnesses had stated about me as a father, yet Rydell seemed annoyed by my constant remarks about parental alienation. My daughter was spending more time with the fathers of her friends (was Rydell going to examine them?) than she was with me. Soon I would be in London working for two months. I was anxious to see some sign from Robbins that she would step in and rectify some of these issues before I had to leave. I literally started to panic. I looked at the whole picture and wondered how it had been allowed to get this way and how anyone could rightly say that this was in the best interest of the child. How was this in anyone's best interest, except lawyers, rent-a-judges, and therapists?

I knew that many men who had suffered at the hands of this system were fathers for whom there was never any doubt that they loved their children or that they functioned well as a parent to those children, regardless of what neglect or mistakes they were responsible for as husbands. I was one of those men. In the spring of 2002, people were maneuvering to severely limit my time with my daughter, if not take her away from me completely. Countless men have come forward to share with me how they have been victimized by the same phenomenon. Understanding this phenomenon is the key to addressing this tragic flaw in the American family law system.

6

Parental Alienation

I~~N THE SUMMER~~ of 1985, Richard A. Gardner, M.D., clinical professor of child psychiatry at Columbia University, introduced the term "Parental Alienation Syndrome" (PAS) into the child custody litigation lexicon. The term refers to a psychological disturbance "in which children are obsessed with deprecation and criticism of a parent— denigration that is unjustified and/or exaggerated."[1] Not only does the PAS child reject one parent as all "bad," it embraces the other as all "good." Gardner introduced this term in an article entitled "Recent Trends in Divorce and Custody Litigation," for this syndrome is almost exclusively found in divorce custody battles. Usually, the alienating parent has primary custody, while the target parent is the noncustodial parent. Since courts have historically awarded

---

[1]Richard A. Gardner, "Recent Trends in Divorce and Custody Litigation," *Academy Forum*, vol. 29, no. 2, 1985, pp. 3–7.

primary physical custody of children to the mother,[2] women have more often been identified as the alienators with men as the target, although the numbers have begun to shift to more of a fifty-fifty split.[3]

Since Gardner started the discussion on PAS, debate has swirled over whether it is a real syndrome, or junk science. At issue is not whether or not some parents try to turn a child against the other parent. Rather, the controversy swirls around whether PAS rises to the level of a psychological syndrome that must be treated by mental health professionals, as well as what that treatment should be. Critics argue that children often harbor negative feelings toward a parent, especially after separation and divorce. However, PAS goes beyond what would be considered normal acting out and emotional responses to the trauma of divorce. In PAS, the child's rejection or denigration of a parent reaches the level of a campaign. That is, it shows itself in consistent behavior rather than in occasional episodes or fits of anger. Moreover, the rejection of the parent comes without any apparent justification. The alienated parent usually enjoyed a healthy, loving, and normal relationship with the child prior to the onset of PAS and did nothing that would appear to have turned the child against them. This turn comes, in PAS, as at least the partial result of the nonalienated parent's influence. While the process includes factors that rise

---

[2]Julie E. Artis, "Judging the Best Interests of the Child: Judges' Account of the Tender Years Doctrine," *Law and Society Review*, December 2004, http://findarticles.com/p/articles/mi_qa3757/is_200412/ai_n9471546/pg_19 (accessed May 19, 2008).
[3]Richard A. Gardner, "Parental Alienation (PAS): Sixteen Years Later," *Academy Forum*, vol. 45, no. 1, 2001, p. 13.

up within the child, the core of the problem can be traced back to actions, both conscious and unconscious, by the alienating parent that helped turn the child against the target parent. If any of these elements are missing, the term PAS does not apply.[4]

The level of PAS varies by case. At the mild level, the child does not fight visiting the target parent. However, they will be critical of and disgruntled with the target parent. In the moderate level, the signs of alienation are more overt. The child is far more disruptive and disrespectful. While the child may cooperate with visitation, they do not do so happily. They display almost constant denigration of the victimized parent. In the severe level, visitation becomes nearly impossible. The child may act out to the point of becoming physically violent toward the target parent. At the very least, severe PAS children seek to inflict emotional pain upon the target parent, and may also exhibit delusions of persecution and fear of physical harm if they are forced to spend time alone with the target parent.[5]

Symptoms of Parental Alienation

In his work with children in custody disputes, Richard Gardner identified eight symptoms of PAS. Although these are modified, at times, by other researchers, these eight still stand as the hallmark signs of the syndrome.

---

[4]Richard A. Warshak, Ph.D., "Current Controversies Regarding Parental Alienation Syndrome," *American Journal of Forensic Psychology*, vol. 19, no. 3, 2001, p. 29.

[5]Richard A. Gardner, M.D., "The Role of the Judiciary in the Entrenchment of the Parental Alienation Syndrome (PAS)," 2002, www.fact.on.ca/Info/pas/gard02d.htm (accessed June 30, 2008).

1. CAMPAIGN OF DENIGRATION

PAS children are not just angry at one parent or the other. They are not just acting out their frustration at their parents' divorce. When PAS is present, the child expresses complete rejection of, even hatred for, the targeted parent. This hatred comes spilling out with the slightest provocation from therapists, lawyers, or judges. The campaign is especially vile when the alienating parent is present. Usually the terms and phrases the child uses parrot those of the alienating parent themselves, for this campaign begins not with the child, but with the alienating parent. Over time, the alienating parent destroys the character of the target parent, either as a planned program of turning the child against the other parent, or as an unintentional result of allowing their own feelings about their estranged spouse to overflow into their daily conversations.

Alienating parents often take on the role of the victim in the divorce, and they express that victimhood to the child in statements such as "Your father left us to go start a new family" or "Your saintly mother decided she didn't love us anymore." The alienating parent groups the child together with him or herself as the victim of the divorce. The ex-spouse did not simply leave the marriage, he or she left "us," leaving the child with a sense of rejection by the other parent.[6] As the victim, the alienating parent blames the target parent for every negative repercussion, real or imagined, of the breakup of the home. Some have led their children to believe that they will not have enough to eat, or may end up thrown out on the street without a home, all because the other par-

---

[6]Gardner, "Recent Trends in Divorce and Custody Litigation."

ent refuses to support them, even when this is far from the truth.

More overt alienation efforts include telling the child that the other parent is "sick" and unwilling to seek the help they need, which would allow the family to be together once again. Some alienating parents tell the child that the other parent is dangerous and may well harm them both if he or she is allowed near them. Some answer phone calls from the other spouse in front of the children, and say things like, "That is NOT true. He is a *good* boy. How dare you say something like that!"[7] Even if the target parent is able to speak to the child himself and try to reassure him that he said nothing of the kind, the damage is done. Alienating parents will also refuse to take calls from the noncustodial parent and then claim that the parent never calls, telling the child, "He doesn't even care enough about you to call." The same holds true with key events in the child's life. Target parents are not told of the event until after the fact, allowing the alienating parent to use the other's absence as further proof of abandonment and rejection of the child. On those occasions when the child is with the target parent, the alienating parent encourages the child to spy on the target parent and report back anything that can be used against them.

Other programming techniques include denying the existence of the target parent; labeling the child as fragile, and thus requiring the alienating parent's continuous protection; taking normal differences and turning them into "good/bad" or "right/wrong" solutions; attacking the target parent's character or lifestyle; telling the child the "truth about past

---

[7]Ibid.

events"; or merely being overly indulgent or extremely permissive.[8]

2. WEAK, FRIVOLOUS, AND ABSURD RATIONALIZATIONS FOR THE DEPRECATION

When asked by therapists and other court-appointed professionals why the PAS child refuses to go near her father (or mother), she will give reasons such as, "He makes me go to bed too early" or "She once made me change my clothes before we went out to eat" or "He wouldn't let me eat ice cream until I finished my homework." The child will also use personal characteristics of the target parent as the reason for disliking the parent so severely, giving answers such as, "He makes noises when he chews" or "She's fat" or "He snores." While all of these statements may be true, none of them rise to the level of the child's emotional response. This is a classic symptom of PAS.

At times the target parent may well have engaged in conduct that led the child to believe the worst about them. When the noncustodial parent is the one who left the home at the time of separation, the child can foster legitimate feelings of abandonment. The target parent may also have shown intense anger at the alienating parent, or displayed other behavior that elicited fear from the child. However, since one of the chief characteristics of PAS is its "license with reality," the facts of the matter will be grossly distorted and exaggerated.[9] Also lost will be the circumstances surrounding

---

[8]Michael R. Walsh and J. Michael Bone, "Parental Alienation Syndrome: An Age-Old Custody Problem," *The Florida Bar Journal*, vol. 61, no. 6, June 1997, p. 93.
[9]Ibid.

past outbursts by the target parent. Normal human reactions are taken out of context and pathologized by the alienating parent, all giving more proof that the target parent deserves to be loathed.

3. LACK OF AMBIVALENCE TOWARD BOTH THE ALIENATING AND TARGETED PARENTS

All normal human relationships carry a degree of ambivalence, even parent-child relationships. Children in a healthy home learn that everybody is a mixture of positive and negative characteristics. Most people understand this even about themselves. However, PAS children express just the opposite regarding their parents. The loved parent is the embodiment of all that is good, while the target parent is the incarnation of all that is bad. In the child's eyes, the loved parent is Jesus; the target parent is Judas, his betrayer. The child actually believes the alienated parent is comparable to Adolf Hitler or Saddam Hussein. Hating such a person, or doing all one can to disrupt their life and make them miserable is, therefore, not only natural, but commendable. When confronted with evidence of "good times" with the target parent, such as photographs of the two of them laughing and smiling together, the child will claim that he was only putting on an act, or that he was afraid of what his father would do if he did not smile.

Surprisingly, Gardner and others found that when the child is alone with the target parent, they often express genuine love and affection. Gardner wrote:

> Often, when these children are with the hated parent they will let their guard down and start to enjoy themselves.

Then, almost as if they have realized that they are doing something "wrong," they will suddenly stiffen up and resume their expressions of withdrawal and animosity. Another maneuver commonly utilized by these children is to profess affection to one parent and to ask that parent to swear that he or she will not reveal the professions of love to the other parent. And the same statement is made to the other parent. In this way these children "cover their tracks" and avoid thereby the disclosure of their schemes.[10]

4. THE "INDEPENDENT-THINKER" PHENOMENON
When one parent is accused of alienating a child from the other parent, they usually deny such action and defer to the child themselves. The child picks up on this and defends the rejection of the target parent as their own idea when questioned by therapists, attorneys, or judges. The alienating parent can then claim that they truly want the child to spend quality time with the target parent, but the child refuses. The alienating parent then appears to be even more child-centered in their actions, for they would never force the child to do anything that he or she does not want to do. As several writers have argued in response, no custodial parent would expect a judge to allow a child to stop attending school simply because the child didn't feel like going. Why then should a judge look the other way and permit a child to stop seeing the target parent simply because he or she does not feel like going through with their court-ordered visitation?

Yet a child telling court-ordered professionals that he or

---

[10]Gardner, "Recent Trends in Divorce and Custody Litigation."

she does not want to see the mother or father becomes the trump card in this process, even when the child uses words and phrases that sound very much like those of the alienating parent. The child may even give very convincing reasons why he or she should not be forced to visit the other parent. However, research into PAS has found that children in these situations can and do lie.[11]

5. REFLEXIVE SUPPORT OF THE ALIENATING PARENT IN THE PARENTAL CONFLICT

Children of divorce always feel torn between the two parents. Although their loyalties lie with both, they often feel as though they must make a choice. Often parents add to the pressure. A parent's own pain and rejection caused by the divorce can lead that parent to try to pull the child onto their side. When Mark Tabb, my writing partner, watched his parents go through a high-conflict divorce, his father demanded he choose one parent or the other. "I was ten years old," Mark told me, "and here's my dad telling me I have to take a side, either him or my mother. It was more than a choice of which one I wanted to live with. I felt like I had to choose the one that I would blame for all that had gone wrong. All I wanted was for them to stop fighting and start getting along. How was I supposed to choose? I wanted both, and I wanted them together." Mark, like most other children of divorce, came to recognize that there was plenty of blame to go around in the breakup of his parents' marriage.

---

[11]Walsh and Bone, "Parental Alienation Syndrome: An Age-Old Custody Problem."

However, in cases of PAS, the child supports one parent over the other one 100 percent of the time. The loved parent is the victim, the target parent the instigator. No matter what the dispute (and disputes in divorce go on long after the initial litigation ends), the child always sides with one parent over the other. Although there are cases of genuine abuse where the child should obviously side with the victim over the abuser, in PAS there is no such justification for the one-sided support.

6. ABSENCE OF GUILT OVER CRUELTY TO AND/OR EXPLOITATION OF THE ALIENATED PARENT

The PAS child not only denigrates the target parent, but he or she also does not feel any guilt about doing so. The child speaks to and about the parent in ways that would result in punishment in normal, healthy family relationships. However, in the PAS process not only does the child go unpunished, but the behavior is also rewarded by the alienating parent. The child also expresses a complete disregard for the feelings of the target parent. When told that the parent is very sad because they cannot spend time with the child, the child will respond with something along the lines of, "Good. I want them to feel sad. They should feel sad for what they've done to us." When the target parent persists in trying to make meaningful contact with the child, this is labeled as harassment. The PAS child expresses the same disregard for gifts, child support payments, and any other expression of parental involvement or love from the target parent. Gifts are often returned unopened, or they are destroyed in the presence of the alienating parent.

Often the child will want to be certain that the target parent pays the support payments due the loved parent but will,
at the same time, refuse to see the target parent. Richard
Gardner described the situation:

> Commonly they will say that they *never* want to see the
> hated parent again, or not until their late teens or early
> twenties. To such a child I might say: "So you want
> your father to continue paying for all your food, cloth-
> ing, rent, and education—even private high school and
> college—and yet you still don't want to see him at all,
> ever again. Is that right?" Such a child might respond:
> "That's right. He doesn't deserve to see me. He's mean
> and paying all that money is a good punishment for
> him."[12]

7. PRESENCE OF BORROWED SCENARIOS

As part of justifying the denigration of the target parent, the
PAS child describes negative situations and events with the
target parent that he or she had no way of actually experiencing. Often these descriptions have a clearly rehearsed
feel or include words and phrases not normally within the
child's vocabulary, words to which they may not even know
the definition. In severe cases of PAS, the child will level false
accusations against the target parent, including allegations
of abuse, especially sexual abuse. This is PAS at its nuclear
level, for such serious charges can sever the target parent's
access to the child permanently.

This symptom is the most controversial aspect of PAS.
Critics charge that those who are actually guilty of sexually

---

[12]Gardner, "Recent Trends in Divorce and Custody Litigation."

abusing their children have used PAS to not only get away with their crimes, but also to gain permanent custody of their children.[13] I agree that such abuse of the system is an outrage that should not be tolerated. However, the fact that some abusive parents successfully dodge the consequences of their actions by using PAS as a defense cannot and does not negate the existence of parental alienation in divorce custody disputes. If it did, one would also have to say that criminal insanity does not exist, for it has successfully been used as a defense by those who are not criminally insane. In addition, many parents have lost contact with their child over *false* charges of abuse. Both extremes are equally tragic.

8. THE SPREAD OF THE ANIMOSITY TO THE EXTENDED FAMILY AND FRIENDS OF THE ALIENATED PARENT

When a child is alienated from a parent, they also separate themselves from that parent's extended family. Although the child may not show the same level of denigration toward the grandparents or aunts and uncles, he or she complains about seeing them because of their attempts to get him or her to "like" the lost parent. Even when the child continues to express love for a grandparent or other family member, the connection is broken because their contact with that relative comes through the target parent. In severe cases of PAS, the child's feelings toward the target parent's extended family is indistinguishable from their hatred of the parent, with the justification of the animosity even harder to identify.[14]

---

[13]See Cheri L. Wood, "The Parental Alienation Syndrome: A Dangerous Aura of Reliability," *Loyola of Los Angeles Law Review,* vol. 27, 1994, p. 1367.
[14]Gardner, "Recent Trends in Divorce and Custody Litigation."

PAS and Custody Litigation

Richard Gardner's initial description of PAS in 1985 was certainly not the first description of parents using children as weapons in high-conflict divorce. Nearly forty years before Gardner, psychoanalyst Wilhelm Reich wrote of parents who seek "revenge on the partner through robbing him or her of the pleasure in the child."[15] However, Gardner believed parental alienation began increasing in frequency in the late 1970s and early 1980s as courts changed the way in which custody was decided. From the mid-nineteenth century through the first three-quarters of the twentieth century, family law in the United States and Britain subscribed to the "tender years doctrine." Prior to this time, early English common law always gave custody to fathers. The passing of the Custody of Infants Act of 1839 changed this and established a presumption of maternal custody for children in the tender years, that is, under the age of seven. Parliament based this act on the belief that taking a child from its mother was unnatural. In 1873, the presumption of maternal custody was extended to the age of sixteen. American courts and legislatures followed suit. Granting custody of a child to its father was tantamount to holding "nature in contempt, and [snatching] helpless, puling infancy from the bosom of an affectionate mother, and [placing] it in the coarse hands of the father"; for the mother was "the softest and safest nurse of infancy."[16]

By the late 1970s, courts began to throw out the tender-years presumption as sexist, thus opening the door for fathers to seek joint or sole custody of their children. Rather than

---

[15]Wilhelm Reich, *Character Analysis*, New York: Farrar, Straus and Giroux, 1949, p. 265.
[16]*Ex parte Devine*, 398 So. 2d 686 [Ala. 1981], quoting *Helms v. Franciscus*, 2 Bland Ch. [Md.] 544 [1830].

automatically award custody to mothers, courts began operating on the "best interests of the child" principle. Joint legal
custody, where the child lives primarily with one parent but
all decisions are shared between the two, or joint physical
custody, where the child splits time equally between mother
and father, became the norm. Gardner observed that in low-
conflict divorces, where both parents cooperate and communicate for the sake of their children, joint custody worked
very well. However, in high-conflict cases, where the two
parties litigate every aspect of the divorce settlement, the
children become even more torn between the two parents.
In this environment, PAS thrives, especially when the
courts seek input from the children as to deciding with
which parent they prefer to live. The empowerment of children, by both the courts and the alienating parent, raises the
stakes and motivates parents to try to persuade the child to
stay with them. This only adds fuel to the PAS fire.

Other researchers now maintain that custody issues alone
are not the sole motivation for parental alienation. Glenn F.
Cartwright, of McGill University in Montreal, writes:

> Since PAS is of a serious nature, it seemed reasonable
> to suppose that it would be provoked only by an
> equally serious emotional dispute, such as the question
> of custody is for most parents. However, while dis-
> agreement over custody remains implicated as the chief
> cause of PAS, it now appears that other, non-custodial
> disagreements on such matters as finance, property di-
> vision, or child support may also trigger the syndrome
> by inducing an emotional climate conducive to PAS.[17]

---

[17]Glenn F. Cartwright, "Expanding the Parameters of Parental Alienation
Syndrome," *The American Journal of Family Therapy*, vol. 21, no. 3, 1993, pp.
205–15.

This simply means that the adversarial climate in which the family law system operates is a prime breeding ground for parental alienation. At the moment of separation, a man or woman may well have never given a thought to trying to keep their former spouse from their children. But as every aspect of the divorce process becomes a source of ever increasing conflict, child custody becomes another battle in which one must prevail, either through the court, or in the hearts and minds of the children themselves. The problem of PAS, along with many of the other resulting problems of divorce, would be greatly diminished if conflict resolution, not escalation, were the order of the day.

Because PAS occurs in the overall context of custody litigation, swift, judicial action is required to curb it. An alienating parent's greatest tool is time. The more time that parent has the child, and the less time the child spends with the target parent, the more effective the programming will be. Therefore, stopping the alienation process demands that the child have quality time with the target parent. Swift judicial intervention by awarding extra or compensatory visitation to the target parent often sends a clear message to the alienating parent to stop the programming process. When courts award more visitation time to the target parent, the tension and stress that previously existed between the alienated child and the parent will dissipate and even disappear with time.[18] However, the key is *swift* judicial action. Again, time is an alienating parent's greatest tool. The longer the process is allowed to go on, the more effective it will be, and the greater the damage will be to the child's relationship with the target parent.

---

[18]Walsh and Bone, "Parental Alienation Syndrome: An Age-Old Custody Problem."

Is PAS a Sound Diagnosis?

All generally recognized psychiatric syndromes may be found in the American Psychiatric Association's *Diagnostic and Statistical Manual* (*DSM*). Inclusion in the *DSM* comes only after scientific testing and research has proven both the existence of the syndrome and the reliability and replicability of its diagnostic criteria. Twenty years after Richard Gardner first described the syndrome, PAS is not included in the *DSM*.[19] Critics point to this fact, above all others, as proof that PAS is not real science. However, as one writer who pins much of her criticism of PAS on this issue points out, inclusion in *DSM* is not a purely scientific matter. She writes, "Due to the decision-making procedures at the American Psychiatric Association, politics may affect inclusion in the *DSM*. The inclusion of minority science may thus face higher hurdles to admission."[20] Writing shortly before his death, Gardner felt confident later editions of the *DSM* would include PAS as more and more peer-reviewed research backed up his initial findings.[21] In addition, inclusion or exclusion in the *DSM* only affects PAS's admissibility in court. It does not alter the fact that some parents actively try to turn a child against the other parent.

Critics also find substantive flaws with PAS theory. Carol Bruch, professor emerita and research professor of law at the University of California, Davis, cites five specific holes in PAS. First, she claims Gardner confuses a child's developmentally

---

[19]Jennifer Hoult, "The Evidentiary Admissibility of Parental Alienation Syndrome: Science, Law, and Policy," *Children's Legal Rights Journal*, vol. 26, no. 1, Spring 2006, p. 5.
[20]Ibid., p. 42.
[21]Gardner, "Parental Alienation (PAS): Sixteen Years Later."

related reaction to the high-conflict divorce with psychosis. The anger that such a child expresses, as well as the parent, is a normal reaction to something so troubling, not a sign of mental illness. Second, Gardner overstates the frequency of parental alienation. At one point, Gardner suggested that as many as 90 percent of all divorces involved parental alienation.[22] With this, Bruch maintains that Gardner overstates the frequency of false accusations of abuse, thus impugning all abuse charges, true and false. Third, Bruch claims PAS shifts attention away from the possibly dangerous behavior of the parent seeking custody to that of the custodial parent. This, then, places the custodial parent under a cloud of suspicion, especially if he or she claims to have legitimate reasons to restrict the other parent's visitation rights. Fourth, Bruch believes that Gardner's insistence that the relationship between the child and the alienated parent must be immediately restored, lest it be lost forever, is an exaggeration of the problem. She states that almost all such relationships will restore themselves over time without judicial interference. And finally, PAS proponents have urged courts to transfer custody from the alienating parent to the target parent as the best means of undoing the effects of PAS. Bruch and others feel that such action places a child at unnecessary risk, especially in cases where abuse is suspected but not yet proven.[23]

Again, these criticisms do not address the key issue that defines parental alienation itself. Whether or not the effects

---

[22]Debra Cassens Moss, "Teaching Kids to Hate," *ABA Journal*, vol. 74, June 1, 1988, p. 19.

[23]Carol S. Bruch, "Parental Alienation Syndrome and Alienated Children—Getting It Wrong in Child Custody Cases," *Child and Family Law Quarterly*, vol. 14, no. 4, 2002, pp. 383–85.

upon the child of one parent's campaign against the other rises to the level of mental illness is not the real question, not when you are the one running into walls separating you from your child. When Larry, an electrical engineer from Southern California, overheard the discussion of this chapter between myself and my writing partner, he immediately shot back, "It's real. There's no doubt this is real." Larry and his first wife had one son in their short marriage. From the day of his separation, Larry's ex-wife did everything she could to keep him from his son. Only later did he learn of how she tried to poison the boy against his father, using many of the ploys described in this chapter. The subtle message imprinted upon the boy was that fathers themselves are expendable.

Larry later remarried. He and his wife of more than twenty-five years have two grown sons with whom he has very close, loving relationships. Unfortunately, in spite of his years of efforts, his firstborn still wants little to do with him, except occasional requests for money. The boy, now married with a family of his own, still lives with his mother. "She wanted to make him completely dependent on her," Larry said, "and she did too good of a job. She and I have a better relationship now than we've ever had. My wife and I go over there to see my son and my grandchildren, and my ex-wife is more than happy to have us. But my son, that's a different story." Determining whether or not Larry's son suffers from a psychological syndrome is a moot point. All Larry really knows is that his relationship with his son was unnecessarily interfered with and nothing he can do now will ever get it back.

Larry isn't the only one victimized by an alienating parent. The ultimate victim was his son himself. Long before he was old enough to decide for himself, the boy's mother decided that he did not need his father. Without the child's input or consent, the alienating parent took it upon herself to declare the boy needed only one parent: her. The boy's father was not only removed from his life; she also made sure the boy would never want anything to do with him. Like all alienating parents, she projected her own feelings toward her ex onto the child and programmed the child with the conviction that the target parent did not deserve to have a relationship with him. She convinced him that the father was a man to be avoided, not embraced. In this and every case of alienation, much of the harm is irreparable.

Whether PAS rises to the level of a psychological syndrome is for scientists and the courts to decide. In the meantime, the problem of parental alienation must be addressed. This is more than a legal or psychological issue. At its core, parental alienation is a form of child abuse, for the child is the ultimate victim. The alienating parent chooses to cut the child off from one of the most important relationships in that child's life. As a result, the child will be far more susceptible to a wide range of problems than those who have a good relationship with both parents. Studies show that children who grow up in a single-parent home are far more likely to abuse drugs and alcohol, to engage in unsafe sexual behavior, to get in trouble with legal authorities, and to perform poorly in school. Children who grow up under the care of an alienating parent have significantly greater problems in forming attachments in their adult lives, as they have been taught to push down and, therefore, mistrust their own innate feelings toward others. While children of divorce are also more susceptible to these social problems, the effects are lessened when both parents take an active role in the child's life. The alienating parent ignores this fact and risks that the child will potentially have a more difficult and less fulfilling life. Meanwhile, the child is powerless to do anything about it.

Whatever the reasons that an alienating parent gives for their actions, common sense dictates that one need not see a pattern of behavior listed in a psychiatric manual to understand that this problem is real and destroying the lives of parents and children everywhere. I know a couple whose young daughter died of cancer. Many in our town had made the little girl's battle a cause within our community. We all became good friends, and one day the mother said to me, "My daughter is gone and I can never get her back. That kills me, but there is that finality to it. There is nothing I can do. But your situation is like a kidnapping. Your daughter is out there and you could see her, if not for the malice of another human being." PAS is not just a theoretical issue in divorce. It is *the* issue, and the reason I wrote this book.

7

London

My OLDER SISTER is divorced from her husband of twenty-five years. They have six children together. At one point in the early months of my separation, my sister called my ex-wife and said that my brother-in-law had difficulty finding time to spend with any of his children after he moved out of their house. "My ex lives fifteen minutes away and he has trouble seeing his children. There are six of them and he has all kinds of activities and schedules to choose from. But he rarely seems to make the time. My brother flies across the country to see his daughter every other weekend. Why would you turn that into a bad thing?" she asked. "Why wouldn't you just encourage that?" My ex-wife claimed she had to run and hung up. She never spoke to my sister again. It was soon thereafter that she disconnected all of her phone lines, claiming to the judge that I had "harassed" her on the phone.

It was in anticipation of my two-month trip to work in

London that I met with Judge Robbins to negotiate my visitation schedule for the summer of 2002. The sessions were
held during the spring at the respective law firms' offices.
My ex-wife made her case in an effort to diminish or outright eliminate my custody of my daughter. Kim made her
assertions, and I made mine. The details of these are sealed,
as they should be. However, during these more formal gatherings, the die is cast. The judge is hit, from both sides, with
the uglier inferences of what the marriage was really all
about. Or at least what it was all about as seen through the
revisionistic and jaundiced eyes of the litigants. Now, you
have arrived at a crossroad at which you may find yourself
charged with some rather unconscionable acts, if not outright crimes. Here is where your case inside the family law
system, a civil procedure, quickly morphs into a criminal
case. You are about to be thrown into "the pit," which is exactly where both sets of lawyers ultimately want you to end
up. This is especially true if you have the resources to fund a
protracted litigation. The pit is where someone, typically a
man under the current system, is tossed as the result of the
often spurious charges of their spouse. The pit is the deep
hole you are flung into that only hours of court-ordered
therapy and thousands upon thousands of dollars and month
after month of humiliation can help you escape from. The
process of climbing out of that pit is, at times, inconceivably
difficult. Your opposition will do all that they can to keep
you down there as long as possible. Along the way, you may
slip and fall and be forced to start the climb all over again.
Steve is fifty, a retired police detective in New York. He is
divorced with five children. He tells a story that I have
found to be quite common.

STEVE: Very early on in our litigation my wife accused me of spousal abuse. She said that I had thrown her on the floor in our home on two or more occasions and that I had grabbed her and manhandled her on "many" others. I informed the judge that my wife had a drinking problem and that she was often belligerent and even physically confrontational when she drank. When she was not drinking, usually during the day, she was often argumentative and visibly angry. I told him that she took a swing at me on at least two occasions and that each time I grabbed her arm at the wrist in order to subdue her. The judge ignored my explanation and asked if my ex-wife's charges were true. I answered yes, they were. This would go on to color the remainder of the litigation evaluation, and the eventual trial. In all subsequent reports and evaluations, I was represented as a spousal abuser who had an out-of-control temper and that I needed ongoing anger management therapy. No such therapy, whether it was for anger management or alcohol abuse, was ordered for my ex-wife. Later, in depositions, my ex-wife's therapist was asked by my attorney if she was told of any allegations of spousal abuse. She said that she was but had kept silent about it at the insistence of my wife. As a police officer, allegations of domestic violence could have seriously damaged or destroyed my career. The therapist was reminded that she was a mandatory reporter for such things and was, therefore, obligated to report them. My attorney asked if there could have been any additional reason that the therapist did not report. The therapist paused and said yes. My attorney asked if the therapist "held the opinion that what she was told did not rise to the level of abuse?" The therapist paused and answered, "Yes."

We had approached the week that I was due to travel to London and time was running out. Robbins indicated that if

I wanted to walk away from the mediation having secured some time with my daughter for that summer, I would have to negotiate for that there and then. If I refused to settle with them, I would be faced with lengthy trial discovery and motions that would eat up the remainder of the summer vacation. The other side would run out the clock during any such formal hearings. In this divorce dynamic, you either negotiate or litigate, and both have their drawbacks. Robbins told me I had to settle that day in order to walk out of there with anything.

My ex-wife and her attorneys submitted a proposal that made it as difficult as Robbins would allow. They wanted me to take twelve sessions of anger management with a British therapist and take parenting classes with an additional therapist when I returned. They wanted the British therapist to write a report on me and to have the option to recommend more sessions of anger management back in the United States. At one point, one of my attorneys reported to me that Judy Bogen, one of Kim's lawyers, began to mist over during a particular exchange. When asked what was wrong, Bogen said, "I represented Nicole Brown Simpson during one of her cases and when I think about what we might have done." When this was related to me, I thought it was appalling. To invoke the Simpson case during my proceedings was outrageous but soon became pro forma for Hersh and Bogen. To say that these two were an almost inconceivably cartoon depiction of divorce lawyers is being kind.

Robbins, in my opinion, could have found a way to circumvent much of this, but in the overwhelmingly compromised and defective dynamic of California family law, she presented their demands to me as a fait accompli. This also marked the beginning of another phenomenon I witnessed, which is that the court dishes out all they think you can take. If you appear to be a capable, durable, and fairly intelligent individual, the judge will potentially bury you in obligations and orders. If you appear weak, fragile, or compromised emotionally, you get a pass. The stronger you are, the more you get whacked. I headed to London to work on a television film I was producing, and before the plane even landed, I was already having an awful time.

PRIOR TO HEADING TO LONDON, I was excited to be working with Ben Bolt, a well-regarded director in the U.K., and the son of acclaimed British screenwriter Sir Robert Bolt. I was also excited by the prospect of working in London, which I had never done before. However, the burden of attending the agreed-upon therapy sessions colored the whole experience. To meet my obligation, I would have to see the designated therapist twice a week while I was shooting. The therapist was not available on weekends, when I had abundant free time. The order stipulated that if I did not complete the sessions, I would lose my entire 2002 summer visitation. As was the case before and would be numerous times in the future, I had to hold confidential meetings with the film's producers to inform them of my situation. I had to impress upon them the importance of my obligation (which I left somewhat vague) and ask that they schedule the film accordingly. They offered all the help they could and promised to accommodate me.

The therapist that was chosen was a man we will call Mike Hunter, whose office was in the Kentish Town section of London, quite a distance from my hotel in Mayfair. It was a bit of a haul. Hunter's office was a nondescript building and Hunter, small and soft-spoken, was a nondescript man. My first contact with Hunter was over the phone while I explained to him my scheduling dilemma. Hunter said that he saw no reason why we could not find a way to complete the requirements, and that he would also do his best to help me.

In my hotel room early during the trip, my attorney called. Vicki Greene said that my ex-wife had filed her formal divorce declaration with the court. Vicki asked if I wanted it sent to London while I was working or if I wanted to wait to read it when I returned. She hesitated and then said, "I think that this is pretty harsh. You might not want to read this while you're working." I told Vicki to send it. I received the FedEx the next day and I sat in my hotel room and read the documents the moment they arrived. The feeling that came over me was unique, to say the least. As it was when I had been served papers on Fifty-third Street a year before, and as it was when all of the phones were turned off in the previous weeks, reading her statement carried a considerable sting. Then the sting subsided and the words just pushed me further and further down. Other men have shared with me the experience of confronting the "renunciation" declaration. In this document, one spouse renounces the entire marriage in the bitterest and clearest language possible. Paragraphs contain phrases like "I never loved this person the entire time we were together," or "I was trying to get out of my marriage for a long time but was afraid what he would do to me." To recognize that your relationship with your wife and the mother of your child is over is difficult to do. To read that this person never loved you throughout the marriage and viewed the entire relationship as a painful endurance test is alternately shocking and depressing. Vicki explained that, in such cases, declarations such as these may backfire on the author, as they only prove that the party is, at least, prone to overemotionalizing or distorting the issues or, at worst, that the author is an outright liar.

I immediately sat down and began drafting my response declaration on my computer. To this day, I view the comparison and contrast between the two documents as the most telling evidence as to who these two people are. My ex-wife's document was negative in the extreme. It sought to paint a portrait of me based upon my worst behavior during the marriage. Some of what was stated was outright false. More of it was an unfair distortion. There was not one positive statement about me as a husband, father, or human being in the entire filing. In my own declaration, I sought to appear more balanced. I wrote of how sad I was that it had come to this. I wrote of what my ex-wife had actually taught me about animal rights and how I appreciated her observations about our business. I attempted to convey that I not only did not view my marriage as a mistake, but that I also thought that such assertions, in our case, were unhealthy and the sign of an alienating nature. Such statements should be weighed as such by judges and therapists.

After reading the declaration, I had to gather myself together and go to work. I approached the shoot with a combination of my normal anticipation mixed with a large dose of sadness and fear. I quickly began applying pressure, as I would eventually do time and again, on the producers to compress my schedule so that I could meet my obligations to the court back home. However, in this case I was one of the producers, and I sensed that my need to dash out of there so often was rather off-putting to the director and some of the others involved. Shooting the movie was not the goal, in my mind. Getting to Hunter's office and making all twelve appointments was the goal. Over the phone, Hunter and his secretary seemed more than accommodating. Very soon, that appeared to change. Where initially Hunter advertised that he would work with me to help complete the program, eventually his office returned my calls a little more slowly. Hunter had assured me that once I had the film's schedule in hand, he would then attempt to schedule my appointments that week. Sometimes, however, I had the film schedule in place and no response from Hunter. I had the film producers offering their help, but could not get Hunter on the phone. The frustration was intense as I attempted to act in the film at the same time.

Hunter's actual sessions were relatively without incident. He handed over materials for me to read, as well as workbooks. He discussed acronyms for all sorts of inappropriate behavior and how to avoid it. Hunter was serious and humorless, and like all therapists who are charged with evaluating the behavior of adults in custody disputes, he had one mantra. He wanted you to accept responsibility for whatever you had done that landed you in his office and he wanted you to do it over and over again until he believed you. Like a convict before a parole board, any mitigating circumstances, claims of innocence, and your need to present evidence to that fact only backfire on you. You are guilty, according to the system, or you wouldn't be there. Actually, in the case of court-ordered therapists like Hunter, you are presumed guilty because it is easier and more lucrative for them. You get divorced, you are charged with anger management issues, you get sentenced to (or negotiate for) therapy, and you walk in and are expected to just take it. Hunter had no interest in hearing my side, no interest in hearing what made me angry or how I viewed any of it. Hunter wanted me to memorize acronyms, and if I spouted them back to him, I was on my way to "recovery," in his trained mind. Hunter's program punished those who went through it with an abundance of pride. However, Hunter's own pride got in the way on one occasion. At one session, I remarked about how hard this was all becoming and said that I was sure that if Tom Cruise were in my position, he would be holding these sessions in his hotel suite and not schlepping out to Kentish Town after a long day of work. Hunter bristled and took offense. Did I feel that his operation, the work he was doing and the facilities he was performing them in, were beneath me? No, I said. It was simply inconvenient.

After we were nearly done, Hunter informed me that he did not think I had worked sufficiently hard at understanding his program. He said that he was unsure that I had thoroughly and convincingly understood how I was responsible for what I had said and done during my marriage. I remember sitting there and thinking, *This is the paradox of anger management therapy. Some cog like Hunter, who holds all of the cards in terms of my visitation with my daughter at this point, is doing his level best to make me angry.* Hunter said he was unclear as to whether he could recommend to the judge that I had complied (although eventually he would), as I had spent so much time "passing the blame" for my behavior on to my ex-wife. I was scared. I had broken my back trying to attend these sessions. I had sought to be both penitent and honest at the same time. I finished my last session with Hunter on a Saturday, which we had squeezed in just as I was about to leave to go home. Hunter, who was perhaps one of the least self-aware therapists I had ever met, looked at me as we parted and said, "How about a hug?" I was mildly stunned and said, "I'm sorry?" Hunter said, "We've been through a lot together and I think we should end this on a positive note." Now, at the final buzzer, empathy and fellowship had entered Mike Hunter's office in time for me to make him feel better about himself. It was like, "Hey, I'm not all bad, am I?"

I walked out of Hunter's office and reached a nearby corner. I leaned against the plywood barriers of a construction site, covered in British billboards for unfamiliar music acts, and paused there in the midday sun. All of the fear and all of the sick feelings I had carried with me since Robbins allowed this insanity to go forward overtook me now. I broke down sobbing on the streets of Kentish Town, outside of London. Hersh, Bogen, and Kim had made it all as unspeakably humiliating as they possibly could, but I had made it. I made it even though the experience of shooting the film was compromised and any pleasure I might have taken in working in London for six weeks was lost. I had made it. I was willing to sacrifice anything in order to save my right to parent my child. I would sacrifice my work, my own comfort. Eventually, I would sacrifice my own physical health and, at times, my own sanity. I see, in retrospect, that this is the juncture where I crossed a line. As I stood there crying and feeling the elation that I had prevailed in that round, I see now that I had fully entered the realm of confrontation and obsession to which the system hopes you will go. You are at war and want to win. And although you are right to want to win the battle for your child, that battle overtakes your entire life. It becomes your life. And then it ruins your life. I thought I was going home to be rewarded for what I had accomplished. Instead, Hersh and Kim were just getting started.

8

Not the Sharpest Knife

WHEN I RETURNED from London, I was anxious to move forward. I was eager to get started with the summer visitation that I believed I had qualified for as the result of my twelve sessions with Hunter. In meetings with Robbins, Hunter's report was ultimately introduced and, as with Rydell, the custody evaluator, the level of honesty I had displayed with Hunter had backfired somewhat. Essentially, Hunter said that I was angry. He did, indeed, pass the jug (a term I use to describe recommending further therapy sessions with a therapeutic or legal colleague) and suggested that I needed other sessions with a U.S. therapist. I contacted a man we will call Mike Goodman in Los Angeles. Goodman, in the sessions I would eventually conduct with him, became "Good Mike," as a counterpoint to Hunter. I would eventually have a handful of sessions with Goodman and he would prove to be quite helpful with my case.

Mike Goodman is a middle-aged, Topanga Canyon hippie

type with a ponytail and Birkenstocks. His office is, strangely, in a small complex off the beaten path near Santa Monica. It's not Kentish Town, but like Bad Mike, Good Mike operated on the fringe of other court-appointed therapists, not the big-ticket shrinks in Beverly Hills or at Cedars Sinai, for example. However, Good Mike began the sessions with the welcome acknowledgment that anger, in and of itself, is not bad or wrong. To be angry, at appropriate times and under appropriate provocation, is normal, even healthy. Goodman taught me that retaliation is the issue. If someone does something to piss you off and you take the bait and respond, they win. It sounds so simple now, but I had made that mistake over and over again. Goodman taught me to run away. "You want to stay in the argument and make your point," he said. "In a marriage, you care so much about what this person thinks of you. We always do. That's why we stay and fight. If we didn't care, we wouldn't bother. You have to learn that by walking away, by protecting yourself, that doesn't mean you don't care. When things get too ugly, walk away."

I will never forget what Good Mike said. Don't retaliate. Walk away. In some cases, run away. Goodman also talked about the alienation factor in high-conflict divorces and how many litigants, especially woman, sought to pathologize certain male behavior that they once appreciated in their husbands. Steve's divorce proceedings were overwhelmed by charges of anger issues and verbal abuse that played out in a way that is more common than one might imagine:

STEVE: My wife used to always say that she felt safe with me. That she knew I could protect her if we were ever threatened. We would walk the streets of New York City and she said that she liked that I wasn't afraid of anyone. Once some guy hit on my wife at her gym. She asked him to "give her some privacy" in a lounge at the facility, but he persisted and, she claimed, he put his hand on her. I was upset about it but didn't want to overreact. Maybe she misunderstood what he meant? But she was incensed. A few months later, we ran into the guy at a restaurant in New York. It was odd, and she kept saying, "What are you going to do?" I waited outside for the guy to finish dinner while my wife sat at the bar. When he came out, I pointed to her and asked if he recognized her. He obviously knew what it was about, because he had been staring at us during dinner for about an hour. I told him that if he ever came near her again, I would bust him up so badly, he would leave town. Eventually, he quit the gym and never came back. Later, during the divorce, she used this as an example of my "uncontrolled anger problem."

Goodman said that there are people he had observed during his practice that he termed the "objective negative function." Sometimes, these people are consumed by such extreme narcissism that they are wholly incapable of considering another's point of view. If you are in a relationship with such a person, a person who literally holds to a "my way or the highway" belief, you are going to be in a near perpetual state of frustration and, ultimately, anger. "The objective negative function is actually anything that destroys without prejudice. Like fire or a hurricane, such people destroy what is in front of them because that is their nature. It is what they do. They can't help it. They actually do not have a mind of their own. This is true of very narcissistic people.

And the people in their lives, those that choose to stay, often develop anger problems."

The other condition of the summer visitation was that I attend parenting classes with a Los Angeles therapist named Jane Shatz. As it was explained to me, Shatz was to help me learn "child-centered" behavior. My sessions with her would become perhaps the most valuable I had throughout the entire experience. I believe that had my case been overseen by someone as intelligent, honest, and reasonable as Jane Shatz, my whole nightmare might have ended a lot sooner. Shatz is one of the heroes of the story.

Jane is a soft-spoken and soothing woman. She sat and listened patiently and with real empathy as I told her how I ended up in her office. Jane taught me two fundamental ideas in our time together. One is that all behavior is consistent. This means that, typically, the way that the litigants behave during the divorce proceedings is a good indicator as to how they behaved during the marriage. It also means that claims that are made during the divorce should be weighed against the past and ongoing behavior of the litigants. If a litigant claims that their spouse was abusive in any way during the marriage, this should be investigated with an eye toward the past behavior of the accused. As Shatz told me, people don't start abusing their spouses late in life. Men typically don't start hitting their wives in their forties. There is normally a discernible pattern of such behavior that predates the marriage. Such claims could be viewed as elements of a potential campaign of alienation.

Jane Shatz also taught me that children in divorce do some amazing things in order to protect themselves, particularly when the pressures of alienation are exerted on them. A mother that is attempting to alienate a child from the child's father sends signals to the child. These signals are not only that nearly any love for or loyalty toward the father is an act of betrayal, but also that the child is significantly responsible for the mother's emotional well-being. These children become caretakers of the alienating parent. A form of emotional incest is evident. The child knows, instinctively, that it has little choice but to please the custodial parent. The child's very life becomes, in a sense, about pleasing the alienating parent within the divorce matrix.

The noncustodial parent, usually the father, is thus expected to endure a steady diet of missed phone calls, little acknowledgment of significant dates like Father's Day or birthdays. There is also a palpable sense that, while the child is in the mother's magnetic field, the father should expect the relationship to survive on very few actual exchanges of the feelings and ideas that normally exist between a parent and child. "She knows you will always be there, so she takes that for granted," Shatz said. "She must always be worried about someone else. She is busy dealing with the pressure from the other side. She just assumes you know that she has no choice and that you will understand." Right away I thought of those news reports with videos of Westerners forced to speak against their country with a rifle to their head. Suddenly, the dilemma of the alienated child was becoming a little clearer to me.

In the subsequent hearings with Robbins, I was awarded a supervised visitation with my daughter. My ex-wife had successfully argued that my daughter would be uncomfortable traveling alone with me to New York for two weeks at the age of six. I offered to hire a woman to tend to my daughter's needs while we were away. I also asked if one of my nieces, my daughter's own cousins, would be suitable to travel with us. However, my ex-wife argued that the child would be better served by having her own nanny accompany her. I was left with no choice but to bring the nanny, a woman we will call Mrs. James, with us. This woman would eventually testify against me in the custody evaluation. Mrs. James had worked for my ex-wife for nearly all of the time we were together. In the recovery room, after the birth of my daughter, I asked my wife what she thought of naming my daughter after Mrs. James. Kim, who would never imagine that her child would be named for anyone in her own family, never mind mine, agreed. (It was one of the few suggestions of mine she ever approved of wholeheartedly, as I recall.) Mrs. James had been of tremendous aid and comfort to Kim during her pregnancy, and she burst into tears upon learning that my daughter's middle name would be her own.

Mrs. James also had to accompany my daughter during the 2002 holiday season. Things had gone relatively smoothly, although the tension of having this woman lingering around convinced me that she was essentially an ersatz spy. I once had a real fondness for Mrs. James. She was a native of Brazil who had married an American. Her family had lived in L.A. for many years, and she was introduced to Kim through a mutual acquaintance. Eventually, Mrs. James's own son would be embroiled in a custody battle of his own. In light of that, I naïvely assumed she would remain neutral in my own proceedings. However, her attachment to Kim and, no doubt, the urgings of Kim's lawyers turned her against me. Mrs. James's testimony would be one of the most determinative in my evaluation.

AS I MADE MY WAY through the holidays of 2002, sensing that this kind of endurance test might go on for longer than

I bargained, I kept hearing the voice of Tom, my sister's neighbor, who was divorced and had three daughters. His story and his advice to me, particularly at that time, had a great impact. Tom told me that I must never give up fighting for my daughter. He told me the story of how he had been urged by his ex to "back off" and let her advise him when the time was right for him to have eventual visitation with his children. In Tom's words, that time never came. The "adjustment period" his ex requested became the foundation for an alienation program that culminated in one of Tom's daughters calling the police on him and having him arrested for "harassment" when he came to their home to visit them for a holiday. Tom said that years had gone by and he never speaks to any of his three children. A slight and mild-mannered man, he sat next to his new fiancée and literally begged me. He said, "Your daughter will never forgive you if you don't fight for her. I accommodated my ex-wife. And my daughters have never forgiven me for it."

The aforementioned custody evaluation sessions with Rydell began at this time, as well. I think it is worth mentioning that, at this point in 2002, I was living under a court order (although some of this was the result of mediation and not at the judge's own direction), which simultaneously included parenting classes with Jane Schatz, supplemental anger management classes with Good Mike, and custody evaluation sessions with Rydell, all while I was working on the film *The Cat in the Hat*. This would mark the beginning of a profound change for me. This was the point at which I began to give up hope that I would ever be able to work again in the manner I had known.

These concurrent sessions, and the emotional drain and embarrassment they caused me, began to take their toll.

Instead of showing up for work eager and engaged, my first questions for and most persistent needs from the production revolved around how I could compress the film's schedule and make all of my court-related appointments. No movie producers want to be made to feel that the project is of secondary importance to anyone involved. They want to believe, and rightly so, that you are dedicated to the work and that while you are shooting it is your greatest priority. After the difficulty of dealing with Bad Mike in London and the ruination of that film, I was hoping that I could come home and enjoy the fact that I would be working with Bo Welch, a director whom I had known in the business for many years. The film shot at Universal, which was near my daughter, and I believed that this might be the beginning of a time of peace for all of us. I was sadly mistaken. *The Cat in the Hat* became the next in a series of situations that were completely overwhelmed by the proceedings in and out of court.

ONE OF THE MOST DIFFICULT things I endured during these events, if not the most difficult, was facing my ex-wife's lawyers in court and, particularly, in depositions. The "petitioner's counsel" succeeded in convincing the court that those depositions should be videotaped. The first of those depositions was held at the offices of my ex-wife's lawyers on February 19, 2003. To say that Neal Hersh is a caricature of the avaricious, inhumane, garden slug of a divorce lawyer misses the point. Hersh has real power in California family law courtrooms. His omniscient tone and aggressive language, his apparent complete belief in the representations of his clients, no matter how distorted, destructive, or downright untrue, and his near pathological tendency to personalize the issues of the case make Hersh the monster in your worst nightmare both in and out of the courtroom. I had faced Hersh before during mediation with Robbins. Dressed in suits out of the 1970s and brandishing a large gold bracelet on his wrist, Hersh is a simian-looking man who looks like a cross between Gabe Kaplan and Chuck Norris.

At the deposition, I sat across a table from Hersh and Judy Bogen, with a video camera trained on me. There was no corresponding camera pointed toward Hersh, et al. Therefore, the judge and custody evaluator, the intended audience, would have no knowledge of what I was seeing and experiencing on the other side. The camera was switched on and the questioning began. It did not take long before the exchanges became tense, then downright unpleasant. Hersh's general direction was to assert that I was an angry bully who had terrorized my ex-wife throughout our marriage. Right around this time, collateral witnesses of mine were issuing statements to Rydell, for her report, containing testimony to the contrary. However, Hersh pressed forward with his recitation of every recollection my ex had of my less-than-wonderful behavior.

Hersh had always seemed oily and smug to me. He had a bad case of the intellectual vanity that afflicts most attorneys I had known. Since my own college days, most lawyers had always struck me as men and women who were not sufficiently smart enough to become doctors or engineers. Therefore, they opted for a career wherein rote recitation of the legal code and a gift for bullshitting people amounted to a profession. Furthermore, the average divorce lawyers seem to be playing out some personal issues within their work. Hersh seemed pent up, angry, and even malicious during my dealings with him. I had heard that he specialized within the Los Angeles divorce community as the champion of the hysterical female client, a type of woman bent on retribution and who did not have "conflict resolution" anywhere on her agenda. If a client wanted to engage in protracted and aggressive litigation with their ex as a means of punishing them, Hersh's office was a good place to start. Hersh and Bogen alternately tittered and snorted, out of the camera's view, after most of my answers. Even my own attorney, Vicki, was shocked at their behavior. If Wasser was the model of rectitude in and out of the courtroom, Hersh was like a child who had been given a law degree. During the first deposition, and a second one later, I could not help but react to this man and his negative energy.

Of course, this is exactly what Hersh had hoped for. He knew that I had no respect for him, and that came through on the tape. Rather than sit, patiently, and endure Hersh as a means of sending some eventual signal to Rydell and Robbins, I attempted to taunt both Hersh and Bogen at every opportunity. Later on the evaluator, Marcia Rydell, expressed dismay to me at the way I had conducted myself on the tape. At the very least, she seemed to expect that I would have played the game a bit more astutely. I loathed Hersh and that is pretty much all Rydell took away from my testimony. The man that was accused of being overly aggressive and belligerent during these proceedings had handed them ample proof of just that. This was among the biggest mistakes that I would make during the case.

As 2003 progressed, hearings were held for nearly every facet of my visitation. We litigated the summer of that

year, Halloween, my daughter's birthday, and every weekend visit I would have. The other side never once offered a
schedule or plan of their own. Issues of supervised visitation
were debated and whether I should fly my daughter to New
York myself or could assign that task to a caregiver or family member. My ex-wife's goal seemed to be to take away
as much of my time as possible and to disrupt what time I
had already been "awarded." However, no matter what road-
blocks were thrown in my way, I was always buoyed by the
fact that a visit with my daughter was waiting for me when
I arrived in Los Angeles. Whether my problems resulted
from my career, my personal relationships, or the divorce itself, seeing Ireland was truly the tonic for anything. My
problems melted away, as if by magic, whenever I would see
her.

IN THE SPRING OF 2003, I moved to a house that was
closer to where my daughter lived. The first house I had
rented belonged to my brother, and it was a bit of a drive to
my daughter's neighborhood. My ex-wife complained about
that distance and how it would be difficult for my daughter
to commute to my new place. My attorney told me that such
complaints were irrelevant. She said that I was free to live
wherever I pleased and that many men moved to areas that
took their children out of their usual orbit. I did not want to
do this. I moved within twenty minutes of them, by car, yet
the complaining did not stop. Around that time, the issue of
my 2003 summer visitation and whether it would be unac-
companied or not was debated. The custody evaluator's report was due, and Robbins's overall, boilerplate ruling would
follow soon after that. These "full" orders would be what I

would have to live with for some time to come, and I was overwhelmed with anticipation.

Rydell filed her custody evaluation report, and it was not what I had hoped for. It seemed that every assertion made against me was vetted to a fare-thee-well, while my ex had skated on nearly everything. Rydell had clearly taken sides in the case, and she had not taken mine. Often, I have found, the custody evaluator will tilt toward the mother where young children are involved in recognition of the "tender years" doctrine. I had one attorney say to me, "Any time given to the father must necessarily be subtracted from the mother. Most therapists don't want to do that. Most evaluators are going to lean heavily toward the mother unless you can prove something very dramatic. You've got to catch the mother with a needle in her arm, in bed with her pimp, and the kid chained to the radiator before they take her time away." Men can make very strong cases to the evaluator, including numerous, reliable collateral witnesses, and still have no impact on the evaluator's ultimate report. Steve's example is indicative of this problem:

> STEVE: I told the evaluator that my wife had a drug and alcohol problem. I presented witnesses who testified that they had seen how my wife drank to the point of being high, very high, or outright bombed, three or four nights a week. The evaluator said that she was aware that she was obligated to conduct a mandatory drug/alcohol evaluation, but she sensed that both sides were in a hurry and, therefore, she did not conduct one. I asked my attorney to provide me with the name of the state agency that I could file a formal complaint with. I filed a complaint alleging that basically every major issue I had

raised had been ignored. The government office sent back a letter stating that they did not have jurisdiction over such issues. The system is, if nothing else, a self-protecting one.

The summer of 2003 came and went, and Robbins was nearing her final decision. She was already nearly a year beyond her original commission. This meant that after the initial one-year term expired, either side reserved the right to terminate her without explanation. Robbins's commission had expired in November of 2002. Her term was extended merely by an agreement between the two law firms. As she moved toward her final orders, a small handful of interim rulings that she made would indicate that, although Rydell's report was no Valentine for me, even Robbins could see much of what I was dealing with. The other side never, ever, offered any settlement proposals of their own. They simply sat back, said no to whatever we requested, and positioned themselves for further litigation. Robbins, who I felt was lazy to a fault and who had idly watched Hersh take me for a joyride with the meter running overtime, had previously threatened, repeatedly, that she would have to "take control of this case" if the parties did not find some grounds for settlement. Then she would do absolutely nothing. But as October approached, things changed.

Some judges, believe it or not, have real courage. They are the real stars in their courtrooms, not merely pretending to be while attorneys run roughshod over them. Robbins had committed the ultimate sin, as far as I was concerned. She had let too much critical time pass, which allowed my daughter to become adapted to the whole situation. She was growing up without a father, and for no reason, and she was adjusting to that fact. Each visit would require a warm-up period, a time where my daughter realized that life with me was every bit as important as life with her mother. Robbins had let this outrage play out for two whole years, and with so little to show for it. However, even Robbins eventually had enough. Judges can express their feelings and thoughts, indignation and dismay in many ways, and usually through their rulings. Sometimes, as Gary's story reveals, they can be as plainspoken as you want them to be:

> GARY: My wife is a talented woman. She is wise in many things. But our divorce revealed to me a lack of emotional development on her part, to say the least, that I was unfamiliar with and unprepared for. Even my own mother, not the most gifted analyst of human behavior out there, has said that she is convinced now that my ex is the victim of some form of abuse and that she projects her own unresolved issues onto our case. Her assertions are so outrageous and unfounded that even the judge broke from his normal impartiality and let fly with a remarkable comment. We were negotiating some remaining financial issue and the judge looked up at me and said, "Let her have this one. We all know she's not the sharpest knife in the drawer. She'll litigate you for another six months over a piece of furniture. She doesn't get it."

Robbins made a ruling in my favor regarding an upcoming Halloween schedule, one of a few successive rulings she made at that time that signaled she was not buying all that my ex and her lawyers were arguing. Then, suddenly, it was over. Two days before Robbins was scheduled, at long last, to issue her full orders, Kim and her lawyers fired her, like throwing a piece of paper into a wastebasket. We had litigated before this woman for two years. The proceedings had been private and under seal and, I daresay, even with as little respect as I had for Robbins, I thought both sides were headed toward an equitable ruling. No matter. Robbins was fired on the eve of her most important ruling. Once again, Hersh had run out the clock. He had put his ear to the ground and didn't like what he heard. Now, the woman who insisted that she did not want any adverse publicity and public spectacle from her divorce had single-handedly dynamited any chance of keeping the proceedings private. Two years of litigation, down the drain. We were now headed to open court.

9

Raspberry Foam Blaster

W<small>HEN MY DAUGHTER</small> was growing up, and before I was divorced, I marveled at all of the things that women said were necessary to raise a baby into a young child. There are some obvious ones: car seats and sterilized pacifiers, bottles of juice (cut with lots of water!) and sunscreen, hats, gloves, other warm clothes, and, of course, antibacterial wipes. Wipes, wipes, and more wipes! It seemed like we spent a million dollars on baby wipes. When it came time to put together a home to bring my daughter to for my visitation, I knew that shopping and stocking my house with all of these items was half the battle.

I bought the same dishes my daughter used at her home. I ordered blankets she would like to sleep with or just lie around in, DVDs for her to watch, and every bath and beauty product, blow dryer, and hairbrush she could name. When it came time to go to the grocery store, we made it into an adventure that was probably more fun for me, truth be told, than for my daughter. I wanted her to feel cared for, and if touring the aisles of more than one supermarket in pursuit of the right veggie bacon was what that took, then so be it. Fridays were usually Grocery Shopping Day, and if it spilled over into Friday evening, what better way to start your weekend than in the shampoo section? If I did not memorize the grocery list, I was quickly reminded that it was Raspberry Foam Blaster (!), not apple. It was wagon wheel pasta, not penne. It was Dragonfruit Vitamin Water, not pomegranate.

Summers in New York with my daughter, as well as weekend visits in Los Angeles, carried with them their own learning curve. I needed to learn when I was to simply drop her off and when I was to come along. It seemed my daughter was nearly always eager for me to stick around. If she went to a birthday party, I would extend to her the choice and say, "You want me to drop you off, right?" She would instantly say, "Yeah, drop me off and come back." Ten seconds would go by and she would then change her mind. "No . . . no . . . you come with me. Can you?" There was a couple whose daughter was in school with mine. I went to the family's home for a birthday party. The husband is some computer genius and the mother is a lawyer. My daughter and her friends ran around the house, they played games and danced while I stood in the kitchen, making my best attempt at computer small talk. Every twenty minutes or so, Ireland would come up to me and I would ask, "Do you want something to drink?" She was out of breath and responded, "Eh . . . yeah. That sounds good," as if the thought hadn't even crossed her mind. That's what I was there for, I realized. I was my daughter's water boy. And gratefully so.

Summers were spent, for a period, on Long Island. I have many friends there and what I believe is a pleasant life. I was anxious, as I had been before my divorce, to show my daughter that part of New York and all of the seasonal pleasures that exist there. In those summers that she traveled east, the routine that we established became wonderfully dependable and comfortable. Sleep in every day, get up and have breakfast, lie around and watch TV, hit the beach at around eleven or noon, swim in the ocean, lunch with our friends, more bodysurfing or Ireland and her friends encircled on the beach in some Hamptons Girls Club gathering, over to my friend's house for a quick dip in the pool, home, shower, dinner (with the Girls Club in tow), DVD, ice cream, bed . . . then get up the next morning and do it all over again. There was some shopping sprinkled in here and there. A quick trip to New York to see something we wanted to see. I thought it was, all in all, a pretty good time.

Ireland changed and quickly, as children do once they attend school. One summer we were shopping in town and I could not get her to go into a clothing store to shop no matter how hard I tried. She wanted to go to the toy store. She wanted music and DVDs, but shopping for clothes was torture. The following year, it's the same street and the same stores, but with a well-timed hair flip, my daughter gazes into the window of a rather nice clothing shop and her retail career begins in earnest. This also represented one of the constant difficulties of going in and out of a child's life during divorce. You are always catching up. You are always dancing a beat behind nearly everyone else.

Among the most important undertakings I would attempt during all of this was to normalize relations with the parents of my daughter's friends and with the teachers and administration of her school. At my daughter's school, there were few fathers who had the flexibility with their time that I had. Depending on how much I chose to work, I might have several weeks without a usual work schedule. Few jobs can be as consuming as shooting films and television. Time off from shooting meant more time with Ireland.

I had arranged with the school to work as a volunteer there. Rather than commit to every Monday, I arranged to alternate with a rather kind woman whose daughter attended classes with mine. Eventually, after the actual trial, my schedule was set and I would travel to L.A. for the first and third weekends of the month. (Oddly, the first weekend of any month, per the court's thinking, must include a Friday. Therefore, if the first of the month falls on a Saturday, the following weekend is the court's first weekend. It was my earlier inability to remember that notion that caused many problems for me at first. Eventually, in order to be able to converse with my lawyers about my visitation schedule, anytime and anywhere, I learned to memorize the calendar for the entire year.)

Volunteering at the school meant little more than functioning as a teaching assistant, helping the children complete their projects and papers per the teacher's instructions. It became, however, one of the greatest times of my life. After the usual weekend of fun and relaxation with her friends, I loved to see Ireland at school, to see her with her teachers and in the earliest stages of finding out who she is. When I was young, I loved school and I wanted her to love it, too. During recess when she was in the second and third grades I would buy her and her buddies little bags of the cheap snacks they had for the kids. Then I would walk her back to class. When I got into my car to leave, I cannot describe the feeling. I was so happy and grateful for the time we had together, and yet I would not see her again for ten days. My contact with her on the phone would always prove to be unfulfilling, if not downright agonizing, due to the lack of cooperation of her mother. When I would get in that car, it was one of the worst feelings I have ever had.

Most of the people I encountered at the school understood what I was dealing with. In Southern California, divorce is as prevalent as the cars on the freeways, and many of the mothers at the school seemed sympathetic to the fact that I was making such a substantial effort on behalf of my child. The administrators knew better, from considerable previous experience, than to take sides in any such dynamic, but they were kind and generous to me in every way possible. The biggest difficulty was in reaching out to those parents of my daughter's friends who, I suspected, had been given an earful about me.

This detailed story from Gary describes a more unusual problem that noncustodial parents must contend with as they attempt to overcome the effects of severe parental alienation.

GARY: My daughter went to one school for pre-K, another for kindergarten, and finally settled into her current school as she entered the first grade. My final court orders were yet to materialize, so I would visit my daughter very infrequently. When I would arrive, I would ask, as I always did, what she wanted to do. I would ask what friends she wanted to visit, and it was then that she would exhibit one of the earliest signs of hiding her true feelings. She would tell me, in one breath, about her new best friend at school but then she would say she did not want to see that girl this particular weekend. I would ask why but she merely fidgeted and changed the subject. This idea that her mother was actively contaminating other parents against me was a new one and I picked up on it quite slowly. My ex-wife eventually succeeded at this effort, which took quite a bit of doing, considering her own tastes and demeanor. My ex was a professional woman with a serious career in the literary world. Toward the end of our marriage and when my daughter was first entering pre-K, she would speak witheringly about the other mothers who stayed home with their children, shelved their own careers, and idled away their days with tennis, shopping, and ferrying their children here and there. To see her eventually embrace some of these women in order to gain their trust and turn them against me was stunning. She despised these women but despised me more, so the relationship was forged. Lynn is a very sophisticated woman, and other mothers at the school were happy to play along with her. The crumbs and water she served them, brief chats in the parking lot or the errant phone call, made some of these lonely housewives feel better about themselves. After weeks of seeing my daughter struggle, I realized that some special effort was, yet again, required. Therefore, I contacted the mother and father of my daughter's best friend and asked if they would have dinner with me. They agreed, and thus began one of the best and, ultimately, strangest parts of my whole story. The mother was around forty and had two children. She was attractive in a way, athletic and seemingly good-natured. The husband was a rather no-nonsense type, a businessman with multiple advanced degrees and extremely bright. We knew people in common from the art world, friends of his that collected. Our dinner was awkward at first. I was sickened by the idea that I had to "audition" for these people in some sense, but soon the husband began to ask certain questions that led me to believe that others, perhaps even members of his own family, had suffered from parental alienation. At the end of the evening, he seemed to hand down a tacit verdict and said to his wife, "I feel very comfortable with him coming over and bringing his daughter to the house." Very quickly, my effort to "normalize" this relationship began to pay off in every way I had hoped. I took my daughter to their home many of my weekends. Soon I was asked to come along, and after that the mother, Carol, and I became friends. Her husband worked long hours. He was driven and successful, and on weekends he didn't seem inclined to tag along for our second or third excursion to the local mall to see *The Princess Diaries*. I was anxious to have my time with both of my children any way I could get it, so I watched a lot of children's films that I might have passed on, and Carol and I spent countless hours shopping for junk jewelry, as well. I believe it was seeing me in this light, seeing me as someone who so clearly enjoyed being with my children, that caused things to gradually change. My own ego was pretty crushed from my divorce proceedings. I wasn't leaping out of bed wondering how many dates I would go on that week. Therefore, when Carol began to send certain signals to me, I either deflected or outright ignored them. It wasn't long before she pressed the issue in no uncertain terms. After I spoke of what I wanted in my own future, she joked about the kind of woman I should date and then asked, point-blank, if I could ever see myself with her. I had sensed this was coming, but I was floored. The irony! The woman who had been warned by my ex about what a monster I am was now hitting on me! I told her what I truly felt, which was that I was incapable of cheating on her husband, Jeff, whom I actually liked and respected a good deal. Most of all, I could never imagine ruining the good thing we had established on behalf of our children. I liked her very much. I had worked so hard to make this relationship pleasant for my daughter. I wouldn't destroy all of what we had built over more than two years just for a fling. She accepted what I told her, at least initially. However, combined with the disintegration of her own marriage, she began to change. She outright attacked me about a girlfriend I had been seeing, how she was so wrong for me. Now, Jeff would never accompany us, and I began to worry. At the school, a woman who had always functioned as a fair and discreet pair of eyes and ears for me told me to be careful, that everyone assumed I was in a full-blown affair with Carol. I told Carol that I wanted her to understand that I did not want to offend Jeff. She said screw him and told me that they were getting separated. I asked if she had considered real and meaningful couple's counseling. I begged that she take my advice in the hope that she and Jeff would not end up in as acrimonious a place as I had. She said it was too late. She was, in retrospect, lonely and scared, and she wanted a man to serve as a parachute as she bailed out of her marriage. I told her I couldn't be that for her. She began to manipulate the schedule with my daughter. She rekindled her friendship with my ex, who had immediately banished her once Carol had opened up her home to me. Around this time, I asked the court to amend my orders, as I wanted a couple of additional school nights per month in order to effect some changes in my daughter's attitude toward school. I felt we had a strong case. The custody evaluator recommended against my request. She quoted from a collateral statement from Carol, of all people. The evaluator wrote that "although his son is comfortable staying overnight with the father, his daughter has confided in others that she is uncomfortable spending time alone with her father and prefers when she is accompanied by a female who can function as an attendant." My daughter had exhibited no such signs and had appeared more than happy when with me, particularly after she was able to get away from the alienating force of her mother, such as when we traveled. The judge eventually denied my request, and referring to the focused evaluation, the only name the judge quoted was Carol's.

Gary's story is obviously extreme to the point of being nearly comical, but it illustrates the web that some target parents can find themselves in. In an attempt to normalize my relationship with the parents of my daughter's friends, I had to bend over backward in order to gain the confidence of those who were either directly contaminated against me or were ultimately ostracized, along with their children, if they dared to open their home to me. This is almost always one of the most effective tools of the alienating parent: to additionally alienate anyone who will normalize relations with the target parent while they have custody of their child.

THE TRIAL WAS AROUND the corner as I came upon Christmas of 2003. I was struggling to give myself some hope that this next judge, as well as the finality of such a proceeding itself, would bring me some peace. For now, however, my only peace came while sleeping on an airplane while shuttling back and forth to see Ireland. Peace was heading to Los Angeles and another opportunity to get the grocery list right. So I would fall asleep on the plane reminding myself, "It's Raspberry Foam Blaster."

10

All Rise

Sitting in judge roy paul's courtroom, the first thing that struck me was how long ago it had been since I was last inside that building and how far I had come since the spring of 1993. Eleven years earlier I had sat in another, nearby courtroom while Kim was sued for breach of contract by the producers of a film. From start to finish, the entire event was a remarkable spectacle. At one point, one of the judge's staff members was admonished for sending my wife and me a letter asking us for a personal loan. "You seem like such nice and caring people . . . ," she wrote. The jury, however, did not see it that way. They found for the plaintiff and stuck Kim with a bill for $9 million. In voluntary depositions after the trial, members of the jury said that they believed $9 million was a "parking ticket" to someone like Kim.

That trial starred Carl Mazzocone, the film's producer, and Jennifer Lynch, the daughter of filmmaker David Lynch. Ms.

Lynch was a fidgety and unkempt woman who theretofore had struggled, unsuccessfully, as a director. Their lawyer was the Wicked Witch of the West Coast, as we called her, an attorney named Patty Glaser, who bore an uncanny resemblance to Margaret Hamilton. At the conclusion of the trial, the judge, Judith Chirlin, strode across the courtroom and actually hugged the plaintiffs in full view of the jury. Perhaps Kim had relied too much on the advice and protection of her agents and lawyers, but she had done nothing to deserve the outcome that emerged. It was at that point that I found myself most drawn to Kim. I probably never loved her more or felt more bonded to her, and I was committed to helping her overcome that injustice. The trial was a disgrace. It was a *Revenge of the Nerds* scenario, played out to humiliate Kim because she was the "pretty girl who had always gotten her way," as Glaser had stated in her opening remarks. I would then spend a good part of the next three years helping Kim to wage her appeal.

AS I SAT in a courtroom once again, so many images went through my mind: slipping notes to Kim's lawyer, Howard Weitzman; the press outside the courtroom each day; betting that any jury award was likely to be the only income the two hapless plaintiffs would ever come upon in the film business; Kim choosing her clothes each morning so painstakingly so as not to alienate the jury; realizing the extent of Chirlin's contempt for Kim and Howard; the faces of the jury on the day of the verdict. As I cleared my mind of all of this, there sat my ex-wife, across the room from me, but now as the plaintiff in the case. With everything we had witnessed together, I had not imagined this was possible. I began to understand that she might have the legal equivalent of Munchausen syndrome. It seems, or at least it did then, that she was never more engaged or more alive than when she was surrounded by a battery of high-priced lawyers.

I had been nominated for an Academy Award in 2004. It was another surprise I had never expected, but any fun or pleasure derived from that once-in-a-lifetime experience was now impacted by the trial. I was performing in a play on Broadway then, as well. I would travel to Los Angeles to attend the Oscars on a Sunday night and be in court first thing on Monday morning. Then I would fly back to New York to do the show on Tuesday evening at the Roundabout Theatre. As I sat in the courtroom, it occurred to me that now I was in the very bowels of the system itself. No more lawyers' offices in Beverly Hills or Century City. No more pleasantries between rent-a-judges and counsel about travel and fine food. No more running out the clock in the way that Hersh had mastered. We were in Judge Roy Paul's courtroom in Los Angeles County Court. There were armed bailiffs and bored, wan-looking secretaries. The walls were a dismal, institutional color. Other litigants sat nearby with their attorneys waiting to be called. You park yourself in the courtroom with a roomful of strangers, all of whom know who you are and also know some of the details of your case. Then someone says, "All rise," and suddenly I prayed that things would change and quickly.

Roy Paul is a compact, middle-aged man with dark hair and eyeglasses who looks like Antonin Scalia's better-looking brother. Early on, I sensed the difference between Jill Robbins and Roy Paul. For two full years, Robbins spoke agitatedly about the need for the two sides to settle the issues of the case, yet her words rang hollow. The lawyers were like the judge's children screaming for candy at the grocery store, with Robbins threatening to punish them with her empty promise to "take control of the case." In the end, however, the children got their way. Robbins introduced me to the concept of the family law judge as Las Vegas pit boss. In the end, her role was to get out of the way of the litigants gambling at the tables. Her ultimate function was to ensure that the gaming went on uninterrupted. The house always won, and that meant the big law firms and court-appointed therapists in L.A.

Paul did not seem like the pit boss type at all. He glanced up from the pile of paperwork produced through two years of active litigation and a full custody evaluation and wondered aloud why the case had not been settled. He would sometimes look straight ahead toward the back wall of the courtroom or at the clock, so as to avoid giving the impression that his chiding remarks were directed at any one side. (At a benefit fund-raiser in Atlanta around that time, a judge taught me the golden rule of the courtroom: a judge tries not to make the lawyers look bad, and the lawyers return the favor.) Paul had read all of the existing documentation. Both sides had filed several pleadings prior to my arrival. This was a pretrial conference, and Paul's comments were clearly designed to preempt an actual trial, with all of its attendant discovery and depositions that would likely stretch on for weeks. His comments also seemed to be aimed squarely at my ex-wife and her lawyers. Paul, I believe, was beginning to see what my attorneys and I had seen for years. The other side had no interest in settling the case. They opposed any compromise offers and provided no counteroffers of their own. Gary faced a similar dilemma during the custody phase of his litigation.

GARY: Eventually we were forced to conduct an actual trial. By that time, things had deteriorated to a point I did not think was possible. During the financial settlement phase, Lynn and her lawyers had fought me on everything, and we argued over every stick of furniture. A final assessment of the value of my business alone seemed to involve more than one year. During that period, however, I caved on so many issues that I thought the other side would eventually respond to our conciliatory gestures, but no such luck. Throughout the custody proceedings, it was clear that Lynn had become paralyzed, literally, by a narcissism that compelled her to project all of her own feelings onto our children and to demand that the evaluators' reports and the court's rulings also reflect those feelings. Lynn was done with me, she announced, so the children were done with me, as well. Her lawyers offered nothing. Every proposal of ours was met with not only a no, but a raging blizzard of invective. She wanted me to have as little visitation as possible, and it's a wonder she did not seek to deny me custody completely. When we were in mediation, all of her flighty and unsubstantiated assertions as to why I was ineligible for custody played into the goals of nearly everyone involved. The judge, the lawyers, and the accountants—none of them were in any hurry. The longer it took, the better for them. In open court, however, the judge sounded as if time had run out for Lynn. She had been given so much leeway to attack me and to attempt to alienate me from our children and she had come up short. The judge in our case now looked at Lynn as if to say, "You've had your chance. Let's get this over with." I think the judge could see that Lynn was a bit troubled. My lawyer told me that colleagues who spoke with other lawyers at Lynn's firm suggested that even Lynn's lawyers were running out of patience with her. They were eager to take her money. But now they took turns as to who would handle her calls. I kept wondering about how so much pain might have been avoided if only certain people had stood up to Lynn sooner.

Judge Paul listened to the attorneys' exchanges on March 1 and told me he had bad news. He was going to ask me to return to Los Angeles in one week, on the following Monday, to attempt to complete the proceedings, provided both sides would stipulate to a proposal he had in mind. Paul said that he wanted to forgo all of the discovery and depositions, having read all of the other filings. He proposed that each litigant, both my ex and I, be allowed one hour to speak, uninterrupted, in order to tell him what each of us wanted from the court. I sat frozen for a moment because I was not sure I had heard him correctly. As everyone in the room listened to the judge, I could not help but think of all of the countless hours I had prepared, intentionally and unintentionally, for an opportunity such as Paul now described. Walking down streets, driving in my car, the last thought of the evening, the first thought in the morning, interrupting my work, interrupting my life: the chance to tell my side of this story loomed as priceless to me. Litigants are given an opportunity to speak in courtrooms on an extremely limited basis. In many cases, if judges simply talked and listened to the litigants directly, things would move a lot more efficiently. However, as efficiency is not a goal in courtrooms, least of all in Los Angeles family law courtrooms, situations such as the one offered by Paul are extremely rare. Both sides agreed to the judge's recommendation, and I was instructed to return to L.A. in one week.

At this point in the overall scheme of things, I had one attorney. I had left Wasser's firm some time before the trial, after I realized that Wasser was firmly committed to the "sit-back-and-try-to-enjoy-it" school of high-end divorce litigation. I was sitting in a session with Wasser several months prior and turned to Vicki Greene and whispered, "You are the only one in this room with a soul. You need to get out of here as soon as you can. You need to leave this firm and start your own." Not long thereafter, Vicki did exactly that. My ex-wife consistently showed up in court with no less than two attorneys and, sometimes, three. She brought her accountant with her, whom she had a deep and abiding friendship with, as well as her entertainment contract lawyer, a drab toady of a man whose presence my attorney and I found odd and inexplicable. It seemed, however, that my ex could not face the judge alone. The more people surrounding her, the more comfortable she appeared, no matter that every one of these people was on her payroll. She sat at her counsel's table literally encrusted in thousands of dollars of billable hours. I sat with only Vicki. On March 8, the effort was made to strip away all of those personalities and get down to something more real or, at least, real in every sense I recognized outside of the absurdity of a courtroom.

The content of what was said on that day is sealed and, therefore, confidential. The nature of the proceedings, however, bears some consideration. Paul instructed Kim to take the stand first. She appeared confused and hesitated briefly.

Paul, as a teacher to a pupil, offered that, as Kim was the plaintiff, she was to begin. Kim, slightly unsettled, gathered herself and stood up. It was clear that she assumed she would respond to my testimony, forgetting that it was she who had made all of the complaints before the court in an effort to deny me access to my child. Kim is a compelling figure in public. Her signature looks coupled with her quiet intensity helped her to build a wonderful career in the movies. When she won an Oscar in 1998, I sat next to her and thought of how few actors had walked to that podium with Kim's healthy appreciation of that honor. She was a small-town girl who had long dreamed of that moment. She was a true creature of the movie business. For much of her adult life, it was all she had.

Kim's performances in films, however, had a stamp, as far as I was concerned. Kim had made so many movies in which she was the victim that she had lost the playfulness and fun on display in her earlier comedies. On film, she was lost. Her characters cried a lot. Bad people, and particularly bad men, were out to get her, and she had to take steps to protect herself from them. When she spoke on the stand, her demeanor was the same. It was like a scene from *To Kill a Mockingbird*, the one where Mayella Ewell testifies against Tom Robinson, and although I was not on trial for rape, the tone was similar. It was what my friend Mark Tabb calls "the insistence of emotion," where she believed the force of her emotion alone would carry the day. Kim spoke for much of the hour about how she felt. Then she alternated and spoke on behalf of my daughter. Back and forth, sometimes haltingly and even incoherently, she went on about her feelings. Alone on the witness stand, minus her lawyers and all of her "friends," Kim's abilities as a witness had changed little since 1993.

Later, I sat in the box and told my story. At this point, I had been involved in the process for three full years, and not once had anyone mentioned to me the possibility that I had been a victim of PAS. Not any judge, lawyer, or therapist. I talked about a pattern of behavior that, while certainly not foreshadowing the far more serious problems that would eventually arise, suggested to anyone a dramatic problem with my ex and her approach to co-parenting. The trial was in March of 2004, and my own understanding of that concept was just beginning. Not long before the trial, on a flight from L.A. to New York, I haphazardly came across the obituary of a doctor who had apparently committed suicide in response to a diagnosis of incurable cancer. The doctor was a noted expert in the field of divorce litigation who had devised a methodology for uncovering false-positive claims of sexual abuse of children at trial. Where children had been coached to falsely accuse a parent of sexual abuse, the doctor recommended the court take the child away from the offending parent and award sole custody to the aggrieved party. I was blown away. I had never even heard of this field of family law. I recall how disturbed I felt that I would not have the chance to meet this man, someone whose lifework appeared to be exploring the very problem I had been facing. The doctor was acknowledged, somewhat ironically, as the father of the syndrome he had helped identify as PAS. The man's name was Richard Gardner.

After one hour, I was done. I had no sense of relief, however, as I was completely unsure of what Paul would rule. For more than three years, I had recited essentially the same facts, but Robbins and Rydell chose to do absolutely nothing about my complaints. Every unfortunate statement by my ex-wife triggered some motion, evaluation, or ruling at my expense. No matter what behavior she exhibited, prior to or during the proceedings, she went unexamined and undeterred. Another aspect of my testimony and pleadings was my reliance on more unbiased sources. I prevailed upon some friends and colleagues who I believed the court would and should view differently from my family and employees, in order to deliberately send a signal to the court and the evaluator. I did not want to load the deck with too many individuals on my payroll, as my ex had done in the extreme. I thought it curious that certain court officials could not see this obvious conflict of interest.

WHEN PAUL ISSUED his ruling, I saw how much I had to be grateful for reflected in the reaction of Kim and her lawyers. Of the many points decided on that day, the right of joint legal custody was pivotal, and I was awarded that right by the judge. To have an incontrovertible say in deciding how my child was to be raised, let alone the right to prevent my ex-wife from moving out of the area without notice or permission, was critical. Additionally, a right of first refusal was granted, which provided that I could take custody of my daughter in her mother's absence, such as when she traveled to go to work. My ex-wife had stated to the judge and the evaluator that she would rather my daughter stay home with her nanny while she traveled, rather than put the child in my care. I had rented a condominium some distance from my daughter's home back in 2001. My ex complained about the distance, so I moved within a twenty-minute drive. My ex complained still. Later I had the unusual luck to find a furnished rental around the corner from my ex, in 2005. That had no effect. After being awarded the right of first refusal at trial in 2004, my ex still left town on more than one occasion and refused to turn over my daughter, in violation of the court order, even though my L.A. home was now one block away. The right of first refusal is a profoundly important one, because it presumes that a growing number of women work full-time while raising their children and that many of those women also travel as part of those jobs.

Paul's telephone orders, the frequency of and schedule by which I would be allowed to phone my daughter, were oddly restrictive. My attorney told me that he couldn't award me everything, but the significance of telephone orders, the original ones issued at trial, would loom over the next several years with enormous consequences. Had I known then what I know now, I would have asked for substantially more effective telephone orders that would have saved me hours of difficulty and needlessly wasted energy. Both parties had spent nearly one million dollars in legal fees by this point, money that might easily have been better spent, perhaps on my daughter herself. You could not put a price, however, on the time I would eventually spend trying to get my daughter on the phone in the coming years. Paul also recommended that we have a special master commissioned in our case, a court-supervised therapist who would adjudicate the conflicts that would no doubt eventually arise from these orders. Vicki told me that this was a very good thing.

I looked at Paul briefly, and the trial was over. He left the room and I never saw him again. He was transferred to another court and our case was assigned to another judge. Roy Paul was one of the few truly decent figures I met on this path. He was fair, he was clever, and he did not seek to pass the jug. I will always be indebted to him, in spite of the fact that several of his orders would soon be violated.

Kim wept during much of the reading of Paul's decision. I never realized until that moment how important it had been to her to take my daughter from me. I recall that this was the first time I would turn to Vicki and say, "I would never have dreamed of doing to her what she has done to me." Vicki said that she had not seen, during all of her career, a man who rightfully wanted to parent his child who had been treated the way I had been treated. Later on, I met Steve, whose words I will always remember.

> STEVE: My wife and I could not afford mediation, so we were in a courtroom very quickly. During the actual trial, my ex's mother called me to offer her support. She said she was sorry that I had been put through all of this and that she knew I was a good dad. I told her that I could never imagine why Debbie would do this to me and to our children. She paused and said, "Well, you aren't her kin. You're not her blood. She only cares about the children because they are her blood. Your wife, your husband, they're never your blood. That's just the way it is."

At that point, one of my greatest sadnesses was that I would probably never be able to rebuild any kind of respectful and functioning relationship with my ex-wife. The process of the trial had certainly killed that off. I thought of my daughter, then only nine years old, growing up with a mother and father who never spoke to each other. However, every overture we made to the other side to attend some form of counseling was ignored or rebuffed. With the trial now concluded, I looked forward to a time when I could have two things: peaceful and uninterrupted time with my daughter, and fewer lawyers and judges in my life. I had been in court, pretty consistently, for more than two years. After so much lost time, 2004 would bring my first meaningful opportunity to enjoy that for which I had fought so hard.

11

The Answer Is Always No

A s bewildering and unnecessarily convoluted as family law in Los Angeles seems, they actually got one thing right: the special master provision. "Masters," as they are referred to in legal proceedings, have occupied an important role within the legal system for many years, not only in family law. Essentially, a special master is a court-appointed professional authorized to adjudicate certain aspects of a case, after trial, circumventing both the need to return to court and to unnecessarily involve attorneys. Masters hear ongoing requests from either party and referee any conflicts that follow the implementation of a judge's orders. Special masters make rulings and, in some cases, even interpretations of the judge's original rulings, regarding the disputes that predictably arise during ongoing litigation.

In some states, special masters are appointed by judges, but with the approval of the litigants and/or their attorneys.

In others, judges can simply impose one. In Los Angeles, where the big divorce law firms actually run the show, both parties must agree to the appointment of a special master. Even if the judge believes that such an appointment could save the litigants, and the court itself, a tremendous amount of time and expense, lawyers make sure that they have the opportunity to gum up that mechanism. The appointment is for a specified period of time. Our special master was commissioned for one year. In California family law, either party may terminate the appointment at the conclusion of that period. No matter how sane or cost-effective the arrangement may appear to be, if one party wants to get rid of the sanity and cost-effectiveness in the proceedings, California law provides them with the opportunity to do so. They justify this by claiming that litigants must maintain the right to access the courts. This is, perhaps, the most important truth of these proceedings. The courts' rulings will always ensure that you end up back in court, with the mind-numbing assumption that you will always get a more thorough and fair treatment in a courtroom.

The special master in California family law functions within a simple framework. The court issues its boilerplate custody orders. The parties then stipulate to a special master for subsequent disputes involving the implementation of those orders. The court divides its orders into three parts. Part one covers the areas of dispute that the special master has sole jurisdiction over, such as the common request to change visitation dates due to ongoing professional or personal conflicts. If you merely want to request that your ex switch dates with you because you have an unforeseen business engagement, which can represent the bulk of the disagreements in these cases, special masters can provide both parties with flexibility and expeditiously so. Part two covers those areas that the special master has jurisdiction over, but the litigants may appeal those decisions to the judge. Part three covers those issues that the judge alone can decide, such as an actual change in the orders themselves. A request from a litigant for an increase in their time with their child falls under this category, as do orders covering joint legal custody, among others.

Alan Yellin, the special master assigned to my case, is like other heroes in this story. He is thoughtful, soft-spoken, and reasonable. To me, he seemed to be empathetic to the difficulties that victims of parental alienation face. Never overly solicitous, he both understood what I was dealing with and had seen enough of it during his career. Yellin's office was spartan, but at least he had a computer, and unlike the original custody evaluator, Marcia Rydell, Yellin made e-mail contact a staple of our communication. Yellin's commission did not commence immediately following the trial. Instead, his one-year appointment was activated that fall, when our first request for his services presented itself. From the fall of 2004 until the fall of 2005, I had a view, albeit a fleeting one, of how well divorce custody mediation can be managed when lawyers and judges are removed from the equation.

During this period, a pattern quickly emerged. I would e-mail or phone Yellin my requests, and he would present them to the other side. He contacted my ex directly, via e-mail. The answer to my requests was always no. The only exception to this rule came on the one occasion when my ex actually needed the dates switched to accommodate her own schedule. After the other side gave its customary no to my request, Yellin would begin the mediation process. He would ask my ex what my daughter's plans were for the weekend and why I would not be able to take her myself. Yellin taught me during our dealings that the excuse of "the child has plans for that weekend" is not legitimate grounds for refusing my requests. If the child is engaged in an activity that either parent could reasonably accompany her to, a parent should have the right to switch dates. If she has a mother/daughter night at the school on the weekend I requested, then obviously a switch should not be granted. However, if the child is going to a birthday party, it makes no difference which parent drives her, especially where the opportunity exists for one parent to preserve one of their visits.

After the initial rejection of my proposal and whatever questions Yellin had for my ex, he would come back to me and ask if this request was something I really needed. It took a while, but I sensed that Yellin was signaling to me that I needed to pick my battles. Even if my requests seemed reasonable, he could not award every decision in my favor. On one occasion, he essentially said as much. "I don't think it's good for you if I decide in your favor all of the time, regardless of the merits of your argument. If you win everything, they will terminate my commission as soon as they are able." Over time, however, Yellin decided in my favor approximately 80 percent of the requests.

THE FALL OF 2004 marked the beginning of a period where I had a brief taste of what uninterrupted, contiguous time with my daughter could be like. On my weekends, I would pick her up from school at dismissal on Friday, and drop her off there on Monday morning. My daughter was then in the third grade. When I dropped her off, I would stay and participate in her school's parent volunteer program. By doing so I discovered what a joy it was to see my daughter's scholastic experience firsthand. Finally having a regular schedule was a relief. Moreover, I knew that I could request changes in the schedule, on an as-needed basis, and begin the process of getting back to a normal life. No longer did I have to forsake commitments and obligations, even to my own mother and siblings, not to mention my career, because of the destructive lack of cooperation of a group of attorneys and their intractable client.

Flexibility of scheduling is significant in custody proceedings. In the earlier stages of our litigation, my ex-wife said that it was consistency she was after. She objected, loudly and regularly, to any changes that I requested in the visitation schedule. However, all working men and working women deserve to have some degree of flexibility in their joint custody agreements. The presumption that custody rulings must be unilaterally geared toward some fantasy conception of what is in "the best interests of the child" is unfair and impractical. If you are married, you are free to pursue your career and other interests to your heart's content. You do not live in fear of some judge taking away your access to your children for failure to engage in "child-centered" behavior. Married fathers and mothers lucky enough to have avoided contentious divorce litigation are not threatened with the loss of their children because they happen to have demanding careers or complicated lives. Divorced parents do not have that freedom. They are held to a standard of perfect parenting, and anything less can lead to a reduction of their time with their children. In divorce court, the detailed and, ultimately, unfair scrutiny of their schedules that many men and women receive is one of the great inequities of the family law system. For many of these people, there is precious little negotiable time in their schedules, even for their more important commitments, let alone poker nights or watching football.

In my own case, commitments to events as crucial as my own mother's charity suffered as the result of the rigidity of the custody schedule. Additionally, coveted tickets to the opera or symphony, ballet or Broadway theater, even the Super Bowl, went to my grateful friends or into the trash, as I was never able to secure the schedule changes I needed. I missed countless birthdays and weddings, graduations and anniversaries. If my mother wanted my daughter to be allowed to travel at times conducive to fostering their relationship, the answer was always no. If I wanted to switch dates in order to attend an event, even for a cause I knew my ex-wife was likely to be supportive of, the answer was always no. If I wanted to bring my daughter to a special event in her own hometown and bring her friends, and the date of the event was not at my court-ordered time, the answer was always no.

In most cases, the need for flexibility in the schedule runs both ways. Many divorced men and women rely on each other to work out fair and functioning schedules because they have no one else. In many cases, if the mother must meet some obligation, then the father may well be on the list of those to whom she turns to care for her child. Some divorced parents have actually figured out ways to accommodate each other's schedules. They try to function with enough give-and-take, with enough general rules and guidelines that allow both parties to live their lives with some ease and grace. I did not have that luxury. My ex-wife needed no flexibility in her schedule. She needed no favors from me because she enjoyed the rarefied position that women with enough money to afford unlimited qualified child care often find themselves in. Whether the appointed caregiver is a family member volunteering in that role or a paid employee, child care too often enables alienating parents to push even harder.

MY WORK SUFFERED tremendously during the period after 2003. I still had friends in the theater who wanted to work with me. I had enough opportunities, both creatively and commercially, to make a living in film and television. However, acting became what I did because I could not find my way to do something else. My health suffered as well. It seemed that the ability to care for myself, to make any effort to maintain my appearance in line with the normal rigors of show business, began to seep and, eventually, spill away. I had only the energy to work, litigate, and fly to L.A. to see my daughter. The discipline to counter the formidable one-two punch of my litigation-related stress and my age went by the wayside. I had simply given up. Eventually, the opportunity to work in smaller roles, with Scorsese again and with Robert De Niro, gave me some hope that I still had something to offer. Two full years after shooting *The Aviator* with Scorsese in 2003, however, the pressures of my custody fight remained the same.

One morning in 2005 while on the set of *The Departed* (again with Scorsese), I attempted to call my daughter at our appointed time. I had decided that telephone contact with her had to be improved. Telephone orders had been made by the court and there was no valid reason that my ex should not comply with those orders. More important, telephone contact becomes the only means some parents have to stay connected with their child, even in the most limited way, during the long separations that are the reality of contentious custody battles. Where other men need only pick up the phone to say that they were in town for the weekend and would love to take their child to lunch, no such chance existed for me. During the eleven or so days that fell in between my normal visits, there was never, ever any bonus time. In fact, my ex and her lawyers worked particularly hard to disrupt my normal, court-ordered schedule as it was.

Joe Reidy, the first assistant director and the head man on Scorsese's sets, had called a rehearsal. I had already dialed the phone and got no answer. I dialed again, and again, no answer. I was used to this by now. My daughter's phone would go straight to voice mail, indicating that it was not even turned on. I learned to try these calls at the very tail end of the court-ordered window of opportunity. Often, the phone would miraculously turn on in the final five minutes of eligibility. The intention seemed obvious. On countless occasions, the call was engaged right as my daughter was pulling up to school. The conversation was two or three quick beats of small talk and then she would say, "I gotta go." Standing there on Scorsese's set, not wanting to keep Joe waiting, I abandoned the call. I would not allow another film, let alone one for Marty, be overwhelmed by the insanity of my divorce. Kim was someone who coveted her work experiences in the movie industry nearly above all else. She would not allow anything, anything at all, to intrude upon her concentration while at work. Whatever it was, it had to wait, and when intrusions arose, she resented them bitterly. Here I was, however, reliving the dynamic of 2003. It was two full years later, and compliance with a judge's simple orders seemed to be either unacceptable or simply too inconvenient for my ex to be bothered with.

I contacted Yellin, and he proposed a default time for my phone calls. This was another milestone in my litigation. The idea that I would be able to have a second chance at contacting my daughter in the early evening, if the call in the morning had failed or the opportunity had eluded me, was cause for celebration on my end. The other side, however, could only be displeased. Yellin was empowered to make this ruling, and it seemed long overdue. My own attorney marveled at how restrictive the telephone orders were that Judge Paul had originally made, possibly as a concession to my ex-wife's attorneys. Additionally, Yellin ordered that I have a weekend call, on Sunday nights, to increase the surface area of the overall phone contact. I believe this set of orders sealed Yellin's doom as our referee. He was making it clear, whether he recognized a pattern of parental alienation or not, that he wanted to facilitate contact between my daughter and me. I believe Yellin further recognized, as I had so long dreamed that any judge or evaluator would, that Kim represented a worst-case scenario. Over time she never softened her stance toward me and/or my relationship with my daughter. Many, many men, as well as women, had told me that "things would improve" eventually. But they did not. I had been separated and divorced since December of 2000. Four years later, I could only get my daughter on the phone for fewer than 25 percent of the court-ordered calls.

IN NOVEMBER OF 2005, Kim's lawyers filed papers to terminate Yellin and throw us back into open court in order to argue in front of a new judge. (Roy Paul, one of the only people involved in my whole process who had the unmistakable combination of courage and intelligence, had been transferred to another court.) The year of less contentiousness that I had enjoyed passed too quickly, and now the entire matter entered a new phase. When the court's orders interfere with the overall campaign of parental alienation by the custodial parent, no matter how restrictive they actually are for the noncustodial parent, then another, more potent option presents itself. The alienating parent seeks to turn the child against the target parent by coloring all of the rights of the target parent as intrusive or even abusive. The alienating parent seeks to take advantage of the shifting emotional life of the maturing child by highlighting the "costs" of compliance to the child itself. Everything the target parent has been awarded, every hard-fought and precious gain, is presented, subtly, as a symptom of the target parent's selfishness, even wickedness. They assert that the child's life is made complicated, even difficult, because of the lack of Solomonic wisdom of the target parent. The custodial parent contends that they are enough and the other parent is superfluous. As a child grows, begins school, and enters a period of more sensitive development, with its attendant self-absorption, few children can resist the pressure that the alienating parent's urgings represent. Slowly, yet unmistakably, a more insidious goal may begin to emerge: turning children into litigants themselves.

12

No Doubt

As I walked out of a Los Angeles soundstage in the fall of 2005, my cell phone began to ring. I was in town to shoot four episodes of *Will and Grace*, on behalf of a charity, and had planned a special weekend with my daughter around the production schedule. My sister's daughter, Jessica, who was one of Ireland's favorite cousins, was flying down from San Francisco to spend a few days with us. Like many parents in a high-conflict divorce, I found maintaining relationships between my daughter and my extended family to be difficult at best. No matter how close my child may have become to her aunts or uncles or cousins during one of her scheduled visits with me, those relationships would often evaporate the moment my daughter left my orbit. But Ireland and Jessica were different. The two were close and had enjoyed spending the month of July with me on Long Island the previous summer.

My plans with Ireland and Jessica were the only thing on

my mind as I reached to answer my phone. I had no reason to think about anything else. In my year and a half of living under Judge Paul's orders, and of working with Alan Yellin as special master, it seemed we had come to the light at the end of the tunnel. While parenting my daughter as a divorced dad would never be the same as it would have been in an intact family, at least now I had a framework I believed I could count on. My daughter and I had regularly scheduled time together, time that was not at the whim of any other individual. By the end of the summer of 2005, I thought I had finally reached a place where I could focus my energy on my work, my personal life, and my relationship with my daughter, rather than upon litigation. Extending that relationship to encompass the rest of my family was a high priority. I have a large family and never believed my daughter would know them all well, but the chance to have this wonderful weekend with Jess was important to me. I thought weekends like this were important for Ireland, too.

However, everything changed the moment I answered my phone on my way out of the NBC soundstage. The call came from my office, telling me I needed to call my lawyer immediately. When I reached my attorney, Vicki Greene, she informed me that her office had just been notified by the California Department of Child Services that an anonymous source had filed a child abuse claim against me. I was shocked. This represented one of the most abrupt turnabouts in the case. I felt like I had gone hang gliding on a beautiful day and suddenly slammed into the side of a mountain. In the past, I had anticipated such interferences with my relationship with my daughter. In most instances, those disruptions had been foreshadowed by filings and motions by the other side. This, however, literally came out of nowhere. Just as I believed that my daughter and I had turned a corner, just when I foolishly thought that the legal struggles were behind us, this bomb dropped in my lap. Never in my wildest dreams did I ever imagine I would find myself in this position.

Needless to say, my highly anticipated plans with my daughter and Jessica were off. The court took away my time while these charges were investigated. Once again, I found myself in the precarious position that family law often places parents. I was presumed guilty until I could prove otherwise. To make matters worse, I did not yet know the full nature of the accusations against me. It should go without saying that I have never, nor would I ever, abuse or mistreat my daughter in any way. The very thought that any man or woman could abuse a child sickens me. I have no sympathy for such people. The full weight of the law should be brought down upon anyone who abuses an innocent child. Yet I suddenly found myself on the wrong side of this dynamic. I stood accused of what I considered to be an unthinkable act. How or why some anonymous source could bring such a charge was beyond me. My first thought was that they must have been mistaken. Whatever the error may have been, I was determined to clear my name as quickly as possible and restore my time with my daughter. That would not prove to be as easy as I had anticipated.

Within a matter of days, the DCS caseworker arrived at my Los Angeles home. At this point, I was still completely unaware of what I was being accused of. I invited him in, and we sat in the living room. He was a forty-year-old, trim, very quiet man whom we will call Carl. He looked like Ozzie

Smith, the pro baseball player. Carl sat opposite me and, after opening his files, asked me a series of standard questions. We soon began to talk in earnest, as Carl informed me of what the complaint was. Within a minute or two, I was bawling. Carl lowered his head and allowed me to compose myself. I said, "Do you find that people are making claims such as this, false claims of child abuse against their ex-spouses, in order to hurt them during litigation?" Carl spoke softly, nodding his head. "No doubt," he said. "No doubt, Mr. Baldwin. I have your file marked 'Ongoing litigation with pending proceeding.' That's what I deal with all the time. Someone is on their way to court, so they file some charges to dirty up somebody right before the hearing." I sat there numb. Carl informed me that the complaint was filed by what is referred to as a "mandatory reporter." This can be a teacher, doctor, or clergy. It can also be a therapist. Carl was not at liberty to disclose the source to me, but soon that would be revealed. To sit in my living room with this man, who turned out to be another angel in the story, was unlike anything I had experienced before. This marked the first time that an outside authority had been brought into our case. Up until now, it had been allegations thrown back and forth only in a courtroom. The foundation for this episode arose from a seemingly unrelated event more than two months prior, and that gap would prove important.

The charges went back to a sequence of events during my summer with my daughter in 2005. In July of that year, my daughter and I were together for what was becoming our usual summer vacation. My niece, Jessica, was staying with us, and I was sure that everyone was having a pleasant time. One evening, my girlfriend and I got into an argument over an issue that concerned my daughter. Rather than argue in front of my daughter and my niece, my girlfriend and I went upstairs to another room. After the argument was over, we walked out of the bedroom, and my evening with my daughter and niece proceeded as we had originally planned.

The DCS claim painted a different picture of that night. According to the report, my daughter told the therapist that her father was screaming and shouting at his girlfriend, and that this made her feel "unsafe." The use of this word surprised me. To say that she felt "unsafe" was not a normal part of my daughter's vocabulary. However, I knew, from my experience with custody evaluators and other therapists who operate within the family law matrix, that the word *unsafe* is a trigger word that immediately sounds alarms within the system. For me, it sounded a different type of alarm. This episode was the first time that I had reason to believe that my child was being coached. I now found myself in a completely different dynamic of the alienating process. Since my ex-wife and I had separated, she had tried to limit my time with my child. The court, however, refused to go along. Paul and Yellin instead gave me quality time with my child. Therefore, I inferred that, from the alienating parent's perspective, a new strategy was required, one in which the child was enlisted in the cause. If the courts would not listen to the mother, then surely they would listen to the child if she said she did not want to see her father. The DCS charges were the initial shots in a new battle that, ultimately, I could never win.

At trial in 2004, the judge had ordered that my daughter be provided with a therapist to help her with whatever issues she might be dealing with. The court stipulated that this therapy be what is referred to as "safe haven" therapy, which would eventually become one source of my latest problem. "Safe haven" therapy is not only a bad idea in many divorce custody cases, but also a potentially dangerous one. In safe haven therapy, the child is offered a course of therapy wherein nothing is discussed with the parents, with the attorneys, or with the judge. The idea is that the child is free to discuss his or her feelings and fears, one-on-one, with a therapist, without potential interference from or manipulation by the litigants or their counsel. That might work where both litigants are committed to co-parenting their child in a healthy way, but what if they aren't? What if the child walks into the session with this therapist, who is a mandatory reporter, loaded with perspectives and statements, some of which have been shaped or outright coached by an alienating parent?

The mandatory reporter to the DCS was a woman we will call Dr. Rhombus, the "safe haven" therapist appointed to help my daughter. According to Rhombus, my daughter came into her office, more than two full months after the incident, and was asked how her summer had been. My daughter gave a version of what happened in my house that July but stated that she felt "unsafe" while in my home. The invocation of that word alone, as far as I could tell from Rhombus, prompted her report to DCS. I asked Rhombus why she felt that this was an issue two months later. (My attorney would eventually pose the same question to the judge.) If the child had felt "unsafe," would the child not have reported that to her mother right away? Would her mother not have raced into court and filed papers on behalf of the "safety" of her child? In subsequent depositions, my niece, who had been with Ireland throughout the time this occurred, was asked what the child's demeanor was during the episode. Was she scared or crying? Did she run out of the house or indicate to my niece that she felt, in any way, "unsafe"? My niece reported that my daughter pulled out her cell phone, within seconds of hearing our argument, and called her mother to report what was happening. Jessica was asked what the child's demeanor was during that call. Was she crying, nervous, or anxious? Jessica stated that my daughter did not seem distraught at all, that she was chatting with her mother "like two girls gossiping on the phone."

This DCS charge fit into a pattern that had developed of delaying certain motions and actions, by my ex and her attorneys, until they could be formulated into something truly impactful down the line. The pattern seemed to be to wait and see how the child herself could be utilized in the alienation effort. Consider that a man has an argument with his girlfriend. He has the sense to adjourn to another room in order to do so out of the child's hearing. The child calls her mother to report all of this. Does the child, who will later be represented to child abuse authorities as "unsafe," pack her bags and leave? Were any papers served, in the intervening weeks, admonishing the father for the episode or making any note of the "unsafe" conditions the child was put in? No, none of that took place. The first time this surfaces is when Carl comes to my house to tell me that, no doubt, men are "dirtied up" through complaints to his department during divorce litigation.

Within a matter of weeks, the DCS report had exonerated me. Carl, my caseworker, stated that he did not believe that what was represented rose to the level of child abuse. Later, when I finally reached Dr. Rhombus, the mandatory reporter, to inquire what had happened, she was reluctant to talk. Rhombus argued that once the child uttered the word *unsafe*, she had to make a judgment call. I asked her if she did not find it curious that all of this had been presented to her in September. The child had returned in July from a month vacation with me and had subsequently taken a one-month vacation with her mother. Rhombus said nothing. She said that speaking to me about the matter was inappropriate and that she had a mandatory duty to report such cases. I asked if she had ever exercised discretion in determining which cases she did or did not report and what were those parameters. Then Dr. Rhombus said, "Kim told me that your daughter has been very upset lately and—"

I interrupted her and asked, "Kim told you what?" There was a pause. I asked Rhombus, "How often are you speaking with Kim?"

Rhombus knew that she had hit a rock here. Stammering somewhat, Rhombus said, "Well, we speak just for a few minutes when she drops her off. You know, she'll tell me how Ireland is doing or how she's feeling."

I let that sink in and then I said, "I thought safe haven therapy was all about no input from parents, only one-on-one with the child."

"Kim and I only speak for a couple of minutes when she comes in," Rhombus said.

"That would be a few minutes more than I have ever had the chance to speak with you," I responded. I felt that it was both improper and prejudicial to me that Rhombus had been having any dialogue, of whatever length, with my ex-wife while I was precluded from doing so. Soon thereafter, Rhombus stepped down as my child's therapist.

*   *   *

BY THE FALL OF 2005, not only was Rhombus gone, but Roy Paul had been transferred, and Alan Yellin's commission was winding down. Within weeks, he would be dismissed by my ex and her attorneys, but not before he made a ruling in my favor covering the scheduling of lost time, or makeup time, which led to another dramatic occurrence. My ex-wife appealed Yellin's ruling and was turned down. The new judge, a woman named Maren Nelson, ordered my ex to comply with Yellin's ruling, but she did not. I went to her home to pick up my daughter on a Friday night, and they were not there. My lawyer instructed me to call the LAPD and file a complaint. The issue had just been litigated and the judge's orders were clear. My lawyer said that, at long last, we should use this to begin to build a contempt case. The police officer arrived and was patient, polite, and helpful. He told me that I might want to have him return on Saturday and again on Sunday to ring the doorbell, as each day of noncompliance was a separate contempt of court charge. I went back in the afternoon on Saturday and again on Sunday. The result was the same.

Building a contempt case was something I had never thought was necessary. I had assumed, wrongly, that if litigants did not obey the orders of the court, the judge would punish them. I had not seen any judge in my case ever sanction anyone for legal fees, although at times I knew that was clearly called for. Divorce judges, however, are terrified of lawyers, particularly in the California system. A lawyer would probably have to smuggle a gun into court before someone like Maren Nelson would act accordingly. The California system is replete with judges who wander in and out of the family law courts on their way to or from other areas of litigation. They neither have the skill nor the will to take on the snakes that coil around divorce courtrooms. Therefore, they don't. Enforcement of a judge's orders is à la carte in Los Angeles. If your ex-spouse does not feel like obeying the judge's rulings, it is up to you and your attorney, who is billing you by the hour, to convince the judge that compliance is important. It is up to you, at your cost, to ensure that the court's rulings are worth the paper they are written on. When my ex returned after she had taken my daughter on that weekend, Judge Nelson ruled that there was no basis for my ex to withhold my daughter and stop my visitation. Even though Hersh eventually admitted that he knew all about—and approved—the plan to violate the judge's order, Hersh's ploy worked perfectly. Nelson took no steps against my ex, or Hersh, whatsoever.

AFTER THE SUMMER OF 2005, I saw that the number of days my daughter had off from school totaled ninety-one. I was awarded a total of thirty days by Judge Paul in March of 2004. I went to court to ask that my daughter's summer vacation be divided exactly in half, with the provision that I would spend the newly acquired time in Los Angeles and would not ask my daughter to travel. I wanted one more weeknight for each of my visits. I did not want all of my time with her to be weekend time. I wanted less emphasis on play and fun and more on school and reading. I thought things were going well, so I asked for more time. My ex and her attorneys opposed these requests and offered no counterproposal.

The request for any expansion of my orders triggered another, albeit briefer, evaluation. This is referred to as a "focused evaluation," and it is mandatory. The new evaluator, whom we will call Dr. Van Pelt, was a quiet and by-the-book woman who spent the last minutes of each of our sessions looking at her watch, anxious to move on to her next appointment or simply to go home. Hoping I might have a chance to gain ground through Van Pelt that had been out of the question with Rydell, I asked Van Pelt, up front, what she thought of parental alienation. She claimed she recognized that it was present in some cases. Eventually, however, I realized that any subsequent evaluators are unlikely to overturn the basic recommendations of the initial, primary evaluator. Van Pelt, whom I came to with slight hope, eventually denied my request. During the evaluation with Van Pelt, more things that I could not predict began to evolve. More compromised witnesses were given a voice in the focused evaluation. Each court-ordered evaluative proceeding creates more surface area for potential alienation. Whenever the target parent asks for more time, they invite the opportunity for the alienating parent to attack and smear them even further. Van Pelt eventually made it clear that, like most of the other drones inside the system, she would break no new ground. Her goal was to uphold, perhaps defend, the previous assessment. Gary has a story that tells of how a focused evaluation can lead to an opportunity for more conflict and, ultimately, alienation.

> GARY: My request for more time seemed simple. I had been enjoying a good period with my children. It was not without incident, but it was normal. The persistent pressure for me to achieve a state of "perfect parenting" had not been eliminated, but I thought things were going well at the time. The evaluator's report, however,

stated that my children were unhappy with their visitation with me. They did not want to travel to my home and spend large amounts of their summer with me, although I had presented collateral witnesses who testified that they were well cared for and seemed more than content. The judge denied my request and, in doing so, quoted only one name from the second evaluator's report. That was Carol's, the woman who, a year prior, had been propositioning me to have an affair with her. Carol said that my children complained to her constantly about how unhappy they were in my custody and, oddly, how they loathed my girlfriend, which I knew to be false. After remaining quiet about Carol's behavior toward me (although I did tell my ex at one point, who laughed and said she wasn't surprised), I told the evaluator of Carol's indiscretion but said that I wanted to keep it confidential, as I did not want to destroy her marriage. My children were still friends with hers, at least on their mother's time. The evaluator stated that it was impossible to make such an accusation and keep it confidential. I believed I had no choice but to drop it, even though the utterly tainted testimony of this woman ended up killing my request.

Van Pelt recommended that Nelson turn me down, which she did. Nelson, who would quickly go on to become the greatest proponent of the "pass the jug" school that I encountered, ordered me to come to Los Angeles to attend three sessions of therapy with my daughter to, essentially, requalify for my 2006 summer visitation. I refused. I was appalled to think that Nelson could not see what they were up to. I had asked the court to expand my time modestly. Now I found myself fighting to hold on to what Paul had already awarded me in 2004.

The list of what I had endured had grown rather long by this time. Alan Yellin, in his exit report, had stated that he had not seen a case where one litigant denied nearly every benign request of the other. The DCS case had been dismissed. Hersh had, basically, spit right in Nelson's face when he refused to obey her direct order. In spite of these things, Nelson's answer was more therapy for me. She commissioned a woman we will call Dr. Shackle to replace Dr. Rhombus as a therapist for my daughter and me to discuss our problems and better our communication. Around this time, a friend of mine told me that the court will often pile rulings and orders onto the litigants in proportion to what they believe each can bear. If they feel one is weak, they give them a pass. If you have demonstrated that you can hold up under the insanity and unfairness of the experience, they will just keeping laying it on you. By this time, I was exhausted and had had enough. I canceled my summer visitation with my daughter that year, in direct violation of a promise I had made to myself, at the onset, that I would never let the process interfere with our relationship. All of the arrangements I had made on her behalf, most of which she had once indicated to me that she was looking forward to, had to be scuttled. In 2004, we had driven to Boston to attend the Democratic convention with my niece, Jessica. The trip, by car and by ferry, was one I will always remember. Two years later, all my plans were up in smoke.

THROUGH ALL OF THIS, I believed that the source of the real problem remained unaddressed. That is that the alienating parent always keeps the target parent on the defensive, in court and out. In response to the alienating forces that I had to contend with, I was forced to develop techniques to protect myself. For example, I continuously checked with my daughter to see that she was comfortable with whatever arrangements I had made. This was a by-product of the interference I had endured from the beginning. My ex-wife would call me or inform me through letters from her attorney that my daughter did not want to go with me on such-and-such a trip or did not want me watching her at her dance class, etc. (Although I witnessed other divorced fathers who were welcome to attend their children's activities.)

Many times, I would drop my daughter off at her dance class and she would tell me, politely, that she wanted me to leave. However, I could tell that she did not always want that. I could tell that she had been coached to believe that I had no place observing her at her activities. Then she would say, "Well...maybe you can watch just for a few minutes." Those few minutes would turn into me watching until the lunch break. Then, after lunch, I would be treated to a bit of the matinee as well. The pattern was nearly always the same. When I would pick up my daughter she was usually lukewarm about my suggestions, at best. However, after time, she would change significantly. She was free to relax with me and enjoy our time together. We would repeat this pattern over and over. On numerous occasions, I asked if she wanted to suspend our visit and go home. I knew that the pressure on her was horrific. I knew that her mother had never sent her out the door with a word of encouragement toward my relationship with her.

MY GIRLFRIEND'S FATHER, an exceedingly bright and successful man who has enjoyed a happy marriage to one woman for many years, had offered me some advice that I was now looking back on wistfully. In 2004, in the wake of my trial with Judge Paul, this man told me to let things lie for a while. "Don't litigate anymore," he said. "Walk away with the orders you have and give everyone a chance to calm down. Even though you are likely entitled to more, much more, than you have now, let the wounds heal before you go back into court again." Of course, he was right. However, immediately after the trial, and throughout 2005 and 2006, I was consumed by one thought alone. I sensed that the finite ether that was my daughter's childhood was now dissipating and quickly. Another clock was running out, and I was consumed by thoughts of how things had existed when we were simply left alone, free from the interference of parental alienation.

I was consumed, actually, by the memory of one phone call. It was in the fall of 2003, and I was walking out of a meeting in New York in the early evening. The time had come for my phone call to L.A. to speak to Ireland. When the phone was answered, it seemed like a stranger was on the other end. Most of my calls were made when she was in the car, on the way to school. Her mother was nearby, and there was always a sort of implied monitoring dynamic present. Getting her to loosen up and laugh or converse in any relaxed way took some doing and usually was futile. On her end, I usually got a lot of "yeps" and "nopes" and other monosyllabic sounds. People would tell me that this is just how kids are, but on this particular day, it was quite different. "Will you do my homework with me?" she asked. The assignment involved a diagram and discussion of the food pyramid. As I walked from Seventy-second and Madison over to Central Park, she rattled off the food groups. She was in a playful mood. Obviously, her mother was not around. I walked into the park and, rather than head home right away, I started to walk in a loop around the reservoir. Darkness soon fell around me as I walked and talked and listened to my daughter lecture about grains and dairy foods and cows. I walked around the park for thirty or forty minutes, and when she was done, she sighed and said, "I gotta go." That phone call, unlike any other before or since, made my day. It made my year. It also made my point. I wanted more contact with my child that way. I wanted more regular, normal contact. I thought that this was worth fighting for, so I fought on. Unfortunately, it was another phone call, a different kind of phone call, which brought us to the worst place of all.

13

Leave a Message
After the Tone

In the spring of 2006, I was contacted by Lorne
Michaels, the creator of *Saturday Night Live* and its producer for most of its more than thirty years on air, about
the possibility of doing a television series for his company.
Lorne is a friend who had shown consistent and extraordi-
nary kindness and generosity toward me since we met in
1990. After I hosted *SNL* for the first time that year, Lorne
welcomed me back practically every season. Over the years,
this show and many of its collaborators became important
friends in my life. When Lorne proposed that I do a sitcom
called *30 Rock*, written by Tina Fey, the former head writer
of *SNL*, I was convinced it would be the right move for me.
I would costar as a clueless corporate executive charged with
overseeing an *SNL*-type comedy show, produced by Tina's
character, Liz Lemon. On the surface, half-hour comedy did
not seem like much of a challenge, but my faith in Tina as a
writer won me over, and I agreed to do the pilot.

NBC picked up *30 Rock* for a full season, and Tina's creation went on to win the Emmy Award as best comedy series in its freshman year. My contract called for me to appear in a limited number of episodes. However, I was later asked to appear in all episodes produced. I agreed, provided that I was guaranteed a schedule that would permit me to commute to Los Angeles to visit my daughter. Lorne, who ultimately helped to work out a deal that was amenable in every way regarding my visitation needs, made things easy. I agreed to do a show shot in New York, written by an incredibly gifted woman and produced by someone I had the utmost belief in. On top of all that, it freed me to see my daughter for nearly all of my court-ordered visits. When people asked me why I signed on to do *30 Rock*, I said because of Lorne, Tina, and my daughter.

AS WELL AS THINGS were developing for me work-wise, 2006 had dealt me some real setbacks in my custody litigation. I lost the proceeding to get more time with Ireland that summer, and out of frustration, I did not ask her to travel to New York to spend her vacation with me. The ongoing litigation had begun to take its toll on Ireland, leaving her stressed beyond anything she deserved or could handle. I could tell that she believed she was being forced to make a choice between her two parents, and I knew which one she felt compelled to choose. In cases of parental alienation, it is rare for very young children to stand up for their relationship with the noncustodial parent. Therefore, 2006 would be the first summer we would not spend time together. I was disgusted with Judge Nelson, who I believed was completely overwhelmed by my ex-wife's attorneys.

My lawyer, Vicki, had done fairly well with the mediator, Judge Robbins, considering Robbins's glacial pace. We had also achieved some success with Judge Paul. Nelson, however, was a different problem. She had done nothing to address Hersh's earlier, direct admission that he was aware of and approved my ex-wife's violation of Nelson's own order. Nelson, like other judges before her, offered enforcement of her orders à la carte only. If I wanted Nelson to actually hold the other side accountable, I would have to petition the court to do so. Neither Robbins, nor Paul, nor Nelson ever punished the other side for their noncompliance. Vicki counseled me, after the DCS episode, that a contempt filing was, regrettably, the only thing that Nelson would remotely understand. Therefore, we started that process in the fall of 2006.

The contempt charges focused upon the "right-of-first-refusal" Judge Paul had granted me in his 2004 custody decision. The ruling provided me with the chance to have longer, more contiguous visits with my daughter, which did not fall under my standard scheduled weekends and summers. My eligibility for that custody had already been examined (overwhelmingly so) and ordered by Paul at trial. However, my attorney and I had suspected for some time that Kim had traveled for work purposes on more than one occasion since March of 2004 and I had not been notified. Usually I found out after the fact through inadvertent statements from my daughter herself. Although my ex worked less than she did prior to my daughter's birth, I wanted custody when she was away working.

We made the necessary filings in order to force the other side to divulge my ex-wife's travel records and proof of her compliance/noncompliance. There were, according to my lawyer, some unusually desperate replies from my ex's attorneys, seeking to circumvent or derail the contempt of court process, such as denying us certain records we sought. However, the contempt charge, which carried with it a possible jail term, was the path I assumed Nelson wanted to direct us down. I had no desire to launch us into another layer of litigation. Still, I demanded compliance with the court's orders (which had been issued three years ago), even if the judges themselves did not.

Suddenly, I phoned my attorney and told her to drop the entire matter. I believed we had them in our sights and that the contempt charges would potentially change the direction of the case. However, I also felt that to forgo the opportunity to punish Kim might present us with a chance to improve the overall situation. To reach some reliable agreements with the other side had been a long-sought goal of mine. My deepest desire was for the conflict to end and for my ex and I to co-parent our child without lawyers involved. Among the most strangely affecting things I experienced during that time were the handful of dreams I had in which all that we had endured was over. The persistent ugliness and lack of cooperation did not exist. My ex-wife and I were like any two people who had divorced, yet had found a functioning, mature way to co-parent our child. These dreams were placed at gatherings or holiday dinners where we joked, often at each other's expense and hopefully in good spirits, about the differences that ended our marriage. However, we behaved like two people who were fixed on the more important goal of raising a child, or at least pretended to be. There may have been an actual moment of apprecia-

tion between the two of us, some effort at respect. I awoke
from these dreams with the truest feeling of peace, however fleeting. I dreamed of the end of all of the bitterness
and dysfunction of my divorce. I would lie in bed and think
about what a great gift that would be. I prayed every day
that some form of peace would arrive in my life and in all of
our lives.

Upon dropping the contempt charges, Nelson extracted
from my ex and her lawyers an assurance that they would
abide by the 2004 orders and, particularly, those regarding
my right of first refusal. This was, once again, a difficult
pill for me to swallow. Nelson drafted orders that basically
instructed everyone to obey Paul's earlier orders. It was like
Robbins's previous exclamations that she was "going to have
to take control of the case." I knew that Kim was on her way
to work very soon after these proceedings. Oddly enough, I
read it in *Variety*. Therefore, we asked that the necessary
steps be taken so that I would have custody of my daughter.
Subsequently, for one week in February of 2007, and for another in March, I had Ireland stay with me in Los Angeles. I
took her to school and picked her up each day. We had two
weeks of blissfully ordinary time: homework, dinner, taking
her to dance class. I had fought hard and waited long for
this. I actually allowed myself to believe that this was the
beginning of a new freedom and a new happiness.

THE SPRING OF 2007 had been productive and
rewarding—*30 Rock* received many glowing reviews, and
both the show and I received some awards. Suddenly, following Lorne Michaels's advice looked like a brilliant idea. In
March, I went to London to meet with different producers

about doing a theatrical production. While there, I thought about how much fun it would be to bring my daughter over later that summer. In April I received a call from my friend Scott Ellis, who had directed me in a show in New York the year before. Scott asked if I would be the honoree at the annual dinner for the Theatre School of DePaul University, formerly the Goodman School of Theatre. I hesitated, since I did not have any formal relationship with DePaul or the Goodman. Scott addressed my concerns by sending me the list of past honorees. I was knocked out by the names on the list. It was a Who's Who of many great actors and actresses of the past, as well as contemporary performers, who had contributed significantly to stage, film, and television. I told Scott I would fly with him to Chicago to attend the benefit.

At the event, while talking with Scott in an anteroom just prior to the dinner, my office called to tell me that my lawyer was on the line with some urgent information. Vicki told me that she had talked to someone named Harvey Levin, a tabloid reporter in Los Angeles, who had obtained a voice mail recording of me yelling at my daughter. Levin refused to state where he had obtained the tape, which he proceeded to post on his tabloid Web site, entitled TMZ. I hung up the phone with Vicki and walked into the dinner to devote my energies toward the benefit, which turned out to be a successful evening. When it was over, I accompanied a small party of DePaul students and staff to a lounge at the hotel to have a conversation about acting that was unavailable to us during the actual dinner. I went to bed, woke up the next morning, and flew home to New York. That night, the tape, as well as a discussion of my parenting skills, was all over the news.

Levin had been a correspondent for the CBS-TV affiliate in Los Angeles. In 1995, when I brought my daughter home from the hospital with my ex-wife and ended up getting into a physical confrontation with a tabloid photographer outside my home, Levin attacked me on the air. Levin approaches his job with the sanctimoniousness of a former political prisoner. He has created TMZ as the updated receptacle of much of the trash that cable stars like Larry King often do not have time for during those periods when real news is breaking. Levin, a former attorney, leads a cadre of self-satisfied twentysomethings who jump like rats from public relations sinking ship to sinking ship, giving the world ever fresher takes on Britney Spears, Paris Hilton, and every other unfortunate soul who has the bad luck and/or awful judgment to walk, sometimes willingly, into the cesspool of modern American media.

Vicki informed Levin that the tape was privileged information and that he would potentially violate a court order if he went public with it. The voice mail and electronic messages of a minor child cannot be released in any way without the permission of the minor's parents, she said. As I had joint legal custody, Levin could not release the material without my consent. However, with his characteristic self-importance and a tone of indignation usually reserved for those who have been incarcerated on Robbins Island, Levin went ahead. I considered suing Levin and his parent company, Warner Brothers, but Levin struck me as the type who would only end up enjoying that. He seemed to be that breed of tabloid creature that realized an almost sexual level of pleasure from ruining other people's lives.

The lead-up to that voice mail message was a sadly familiar one. It was another night in another restaurant in New York, and I had excused myself from the table to call my daughter for perhaps the two thousandth time in the past six years. I dialed the phone and there was no answer. As was so often the case, my daughter's phone wasn't even turned on. We had had such a good time just a couple of weeks ago. Now she was off for spring break with her mother and, once again, her phone was turned off for ten consecutive days. I stood outside a restaurant on West Sixty-fifth Street and thought about how I had dropped the contempt charge and how I had tried to improve the situation by offering real compromise. I realized that Hersh viewed any compromise as weakness. I realized that no matter what I did, parental alienation is a force that overwhelms some people like a sickness. When presented with the chance to facilitate the child's relationship with the target parent, which is truly in the child's interest, the alienating parent either cannot see or cannot be bothered. I had dialed that phone for more than a week and only gotten a voice mail. This had happened for years now, and for no good reason. All of the judges and court-ordered therapists, even Judge Paul, had failed to address this effectively. I believe that telephone contact is essential for the target parent. For some men and women, phone contact is all they have available to them during often long and unpredictable periods of noncompliance by an alienating spouse or the disruptions posed by litigation itself. I thought about how simple this should have been and how unfair it was and how no one would do anything about it inside of this contemptible and godforsaken Los Angeles family law system. When the beep came, I snapped. Later, I heard a doctor on a television program say that he could hear in my message how much pain I was in. He said that I wasn't leaving a message for my daughter. My words were directed at someone else entirely.

The reaction to all of this came in waves. The first wave

was the overwhelming media condemnation of me on shows like *Nancy Grace*, with her panelists conferring about whether I should actually lose the right to see my daughter as the result of this single event. Every tabloid magazine imaginable also carried some angle on the story. Internet postings on my own Web site also piled up, written by those who "had always thought he seemed like a bad person." There were those who defended me. Television host "Dr. Phil" McGraw called me and offered to give me a forum to discuss my case. He seemed genuinely appalled by the release of the tape when we spoke. However, supporters seemed too measured and rational to command much airtime. Public discussion of the story mirrored the tone of the case in court: actual fairness and getting the facts right were too time-consuming. I went on *The View* in an attempt to show people that the release of the tape was an insidious attempt to smear me, to no avail. By the end of 2007, many such outlets omitted my disaster when compiling lists of the most egregious media missteps of the year. One exception, however, was the venerable *New York Times*, which made sure to circle around for one more look at the wreck. All along, I could only think about how my daughter must feel.

The next wave was that of letters and e-mail communications from those who shared with me their own stories of how a loved one, a father or mother, grandparent or sibling, a coworker or boss, a spouse or lover, had abused them verbally in such a way that had had a lasting effect on them. Some of the writings were unbearable. Some women told of how their fathers had shattered their confidence and destroyed a part of their childhood with one thoughtless tirade. Others recounted lifetimes of abuse that crushed them beyond recovery. One woman in particular said, "When I heard that tape, I heard my dad all over again and I sat down and just cried all day and thought of your daughter." Again, I thought about what all this would do to my daughter, as well.

The third wave was the inexplicable and delayed concern that people showed for me that could only have come from their own experiences and/or shame. Weeks after the release of the tape, people called and wrote letters expressing, even confessing, their own poor choices as parents. There appeared a virtual stream of well-known Americans, from many fields, all with the same offering. "Hang in there. If they recorded some of the things I've said to my children, I would be put away!" Although I was grateful for all of the support, I knew that the ultimate ramifications that this would have on my case before Judge Nelson could not be good. For more than six years my opponents had worked to set me up, and now they had what they had long dreamed of: the opportunity to allow my daughter's feelings to enter into the picture. If you yell at your child, that is damaging to your relationship. If something as embarrassing as this is broadcast all over the world, I can't imagine how that would make an eleven-year-old child feel.

What came next was the strangest experience of all. The thoughts that eventually came over me were unfamiliar and introduced me to an even darker and more painful reality than I could have ever anticipated. After all of the effort I had made, in the face of all of the terrible and ungodly opposition and moral cowardice, in one day everything had been smashed. I had achieved the polar opposite of what I had sought to create. My relationship with my only child was ruined, and I was powerless to resolve that. I offered my resignation to the boards of every organization on which I served. I immediately canceled every single public appearance and professional appointment I had scheduled in the months of April, May, and beyond. I asked to be released from my contract with NBC, as I did not want my situation to negatively affect the show just as it was beginning to achieve a bit of momentum. I wanted to hide, to disappear. I abandoned any hope that the court of public opinion, let alone an actual court in Los Angeles, would comprehend what I had been through. As I walked up Broadway, on an otherwise warm and beautiful day in New York, a woman in a café shouted, "Why don't you call your daughter, you fucking asshole." About twenty or so people snapped their heads in my direction to see at whom that shriek had been aimed.

My family and closest friends were still there for me, but even some of them had grown perplexed by and weary of the assault on my parental rights that seemed to have no end. On the deepest level, my situation now seemed hopeless to me, as well. I had gone to sleep many nights doubting that I had the desire to face these problems another day. Now, I was sure I could not. Everything had seemed to be improving. Now, it was completely flipped on its back. Driving up the Taconic Parkway, heading to an inn in the Berkshire Mountains, I began to think about what little town I would repair to in order to commit suicide. What semiremote Massachusetts state park could I hike deep into and shoot myself? What bed-and-breakfast could I check into and overdose there? On Long Island, I thought about the old Jeep I owned and the emissions it gave off. When I returned to New York, the thought of jumping out the window of my apartment was with me every night for weeks.

I contacted a friend who gave me the name of a doctor. When we spoke, the doctor said, "What change would you like to see that you think could help you?" I told him that I did not seek change in others any longer. I wanted help with disengaging from my divorce litigation. I wanted someone to help me walk away. "This is killing me, literally," I said. He told me that he had seen quite a number of people who had been consumed by the "quicksand" of contentious divorce litigation. The therapist told me that men with limited financial resources often give up the fight, and their children, very early on. Many patients of his, men in particular, entertained thoughts of suicide in response to the insurmountable injustice of parental alienation and its attendant grief. He said that some men went through a period where they even questioned whether a real relationship with their child, at least on a level any healthy person would recognize, had ever existed at all. "Your relationship is not a parenting one," he stated, "if you are pleading with the child all of the time." He told me, once again, the line I had heard so often before. "You're no good for anyone else, including your daughter, if you destroy yourself." Eventually, this overwhelming anguish would pass as the direct result, I believe, of the love of my family and close friends and the result of prayer and my faith in God. When the day came that I could actually joke about the subject of the phone call, I knew I had moved beyond the worst of it. It was then that I heard a voice in my head say, "Even the deepest feelings don't last forever."

WITHIN WEEKS, I WAS BACK in court, and the legal consequences were overwhelming. Once a minor child represents their feelings to the court, the impact is potentially devastating. During the proceeding in June, Hersh brandished a letter of apology that I had sent to my daughter and plopped it in front of me in the witness box. The letter had been torn in half, presumably by my daughter. In order to put his signature touch on this, Hersh bent over to arrange the severed pieces to form a recognizable whole. Right to the end, Hersh, one of the most malicious human beings I have ever encountered, never missed an opportunity to "advocate" on behalf of the truly angry litigant. Their goal was to show that my daughter did not want to see me again. More than $3 million in joint legal fees had been spent. In my mind, all of it was a buildup to this; so that Hersh and his client could have the pleasure of sticking that letter in my face.

Judge Nelson did the only thing she is capable of doing, the only thing she believes in. She passed the jug. The details of the proceedings are sealed, but Nelson, with her customary lack of insight into parental alienation and apparent fear of antagonizing Hersh, stated, "Mr. Baldwin has come through for his daughter in the past and I am sure he will do so again." She then proceeded to dump the entire burden of resurrecting my relationship with my daughter on me. There was no resolution of who leaked the tape or why. She passed the jug to another attorney by appointing a minor's counsel, never imagining that there were already too many lawyers in our lives. That lawyer, Diana Gould-Saltman, dressed in a garish, Dolly Levi hat, came to court and never addressed the issue of what should be done to investigate the leak of the tape and the role that the leak may have played in advancing the alienation of my child. Nelson made her orders. During

the proceedings, among certain judgments and condemna-
tions I made of my ex, her lawyers, and Nelson's abilities as
a judge, I said the one thing that I thought summed up the
entire situation. "Now we see, incontrovertibly, that the
mother's hatred of the father is greater than her love for the
child."

Back in 2006, when Nelson ruled against me for the expansion of my orders, I was so despondent that I thought I
had become gravely, physically ill. One day, sitting in my
house on Long Island, my doorbell rang. Where I live, no
one rings my doorbell. It was my mother, who had traveled,
at age seventy-seven, to come look after me. Now, in the
wake of the tape event, it was my sister's turn. She proved to
be the greatest friend I could ever know. The feeling that I
should end my life was slowly being replaced with the acceptance that my daughter's childhood was nearing a close.
Many divorced fathers had told me that, at some point, they
slammed up against the realization that what they had been
fighting for had ultimately ebbed away with time. Their children had grown up. Once they had reached the age of twelve,
the "tween" period, children began to exhibit those unmistakable signs that they had little use for either of their parents. These men told me that while straining to keep up with
their careers, their personal lives, the world at large, and
their divorce litigation, their child's most innocent years, the
time from birth to middle school, had ended.

THE SUMMER OF 2007 came and went. No visitation. No
contact. I was convinced that complying with Nelson's orders, the most recent ones or any others she might arrive at,
was futile. I reluctantly went back to work in August of 2007

for what would be a strike-shortened season. That fall, however, I also halfheartedly began complying with Nelson's orders and thus made the necessary effort to help my daughter and me put this behind us. I saw that I did not have much choice. I had not seen her for nine months. As the song "To Sir with Love" enumerates, the transition from "pigtails to perfume" was nearly complete. All I could think about was, *How much of that had been withheld from me and why?*

14

A Trip to Cambridge

I~N THE FALL OF 2007~, I visited Harvard to speak to students enrolled in an acting program there, as well as visit with students at Kirkland House for a more general discussion. My host asked me if I wanted to avail myself of any of the university's other resources, and immediately I asked to be introduced to a professor at Harvard who taught family law. Thus I met Jeannie Suk, a law professor who is a rising star at Harvard Law School, where she teaches family law and criminal law.

When we met at her office, I told her that I was interested in discussing changes in the nature of family law in the United States over the past several years and how I believed men were being treated unfairly by the system. I wanted to know what experts in the field attribute those changes to and what is driving much of custody law today. Professor Suk and I spent ninety minutes talking nonstop, and then the idea emerged that I might come back to Harvard so that she and I could conduct a discussion with her class regarding some of the legal issues that I was concerned with. During our many subsequent conversations, Jeannie taught me much about the evolution of laws pertaining to domestic violence, sexual harassment of women in the workplace, rape prosecutions, and divorce custody battles. Professor Suk's article in the October 2006 *Yale Law Journal*, entitled "Criminal Law Comes Home," is a fascinating and highly instructive overview of how criminal law procedures have moved into family law. Her next book, *At Home in the Law*, will argue that our legal system today views the home as a place of male violence, and that many areas of law are being reshaped in accordance with this image.

A few weeks later, I was with Jeannie in front of approximately eighty students, and the topic was the law's treatment of relationships between men and women, and the struggles between the sexes, from the Harvard campus, to the home, to the family law court, and everywhere in between. I introduced my ideas about child custody and fathers' rights. That led to a discussion in which some students seemed sympathetic, or at least interested, while a number of students were skeptical at best. The discussion quickly became lively and frank. I turned to the broader topic of whether women in marriages and relationships with men are normally threatened by potential violence. Here there was more consensus. I was surprised to hear a number of women and men—many more than I would have expected—say that women generally are at risk of male sexual violence. A few students, male and female, even thought that the law should view the sex act as subordinating of someone and should assume that sex is rape unless women explicitly and verbally give their consent.

I was fascinated to hear some of these law students talk about the world as though men inevitably have the upper hand in relationships and women's fear of sexual violence is prevalent and normal, not unusual. This picture was so interesting and so foreign to me. In my own experience, women have lots of power of various kinds, and sexual power works both ways.

I later told Jeannie that I knew of only one couple in my life who had ever confided in me that one had committed an act of domestic abuse. Furthermore, no woman that I knew personally had ever admitted to me that she had been a victim of sexual assault. Are domestic violence and sexual assault more prevalent today? Or do people simply feel safer discussing these issues because they believe the law will actually listen to and protect women and punish their attackers? Or do ideas about men and women that are currently expressed in the legal system shape the way students think about men and women?

MY INTERVIEW WITH PROFESSOR SUK is as follows:

AB: When first we met, we talked about how some of the issues fathers face in the family law system today might be related to other, broader developments in our legal system.

JS: Major changes in several important areas of law over the last thirty years reflect a series of hard-won victories by advocates for women. This is most visible in areas directly connected to relationships between men and women: domestic violence, acquaintance rape, and sexual harassment.

AB: How would you characterize the changes?

JS: You have to remember, for example, that until recently,

law enforcement really didn't treat domestic violence as a crime. It was considered a private family matter. Also, it was very difficult for a woman to prove she had been raped, because she had to show that she tried to physically fight off her attacker. If she was too afraid to resist, the law didn't treat the sexual act as a rape. A husband forcing his wife to have sex simply couldn't be rape. And the legal concept of sexual harassment didn't exist at all. So the legal treatment of important areas of life in which men and women interact, often regarding sex specifically, made for a very different world—and not a good one for women! A project of the feminist movement was to change the way the legal community and the public think about these situations. And it has had lots of success in several important legal realms.

AB: How so?

JS: Well, the first area is domestic violence. Most people today would agree that domestic violence should be a crime. It's clearly a matter of public concern. We get outraged when we hear about law enforcement failure to punish men at the earliest signs of abuse. O. J. Simpson was an important cultural symbol of this, among other things. This understanding is now reflected in our law. In the majority of states, we have "mandatory arrest" laws requiring the police to make an arrest when there is probable cause to believe a domestic violence crime has been committed. This aims to take away police discretion, since a perceived problem was that the police did not take domestic violence seriously and left couples in domestic incidents to settle things themselves. Mandatory arrest laws command police to treat domestic violence as crime, and to respond to it with arrest—the police are not allowed to use discretion and decide not to arrest in a particular case. Many prosecutors' offices now have similar policies that require prosecutors, even in misdemeanor cases, to bring criminal charges, even if the victim wants the charges dropped and indeed refuses to cooperate with the prosecution.

AB: But taking away discretion from police and prosecutors has consequences, especially in situations where wives are conflicted about having their husbands arrested.

JS: Many people now believe that a victim of domestic violence is not in a good position to judge what is best for her, because her will is surely dominated by her husband or boyfriend, on whom she may be financially dependent. Also, since domestic violence is seen as a public matter, prosecutors see the decision as theirs to make on behalf of the public rather than the victim. They are sometimes required, by office policy, to prosecute even if particular victims explicitly ask them not to.

AB: Are there times when the loss of such discretion doesn't lead to the best outcome?

JS: There has developed a tendency toward the uniform and the mandatory in domestic violence legal practice, because of the prevailing theory that men subordinate women in the home, and that violence is a manifestation of that subordination. Law can be a blunt instrument. When you have a broad public acceptance of this kind of theory about relationships between men and women, coming out of an important strand of feminism, that theory can overshadow particular circumstances, including the desires of the private parties involved.

AB: And you think the legal system operates on this theory of men typically subordinating women in the home?

JS: In many areas, I believe it does. The legal theorist Janet Halley, my colleague at Harvard Law School, calls this phenomenon "governance feminism." It's the idea that feminism, which once criticized the law from the outside, is today actually in charge in many places in the law—among police, prosecutors, lawmakers, judges, and other legal actors. The feminism that often "governs" today is that strand developed by the legal scholar Catharine MacKinnon and that focuses on the subordination of women by men, particularly in intimate and sexual relationships. Her influence on our legal system's understandings of men and women cannot be overstated. If you talk to police, prosecutors, lawmakers, and judges about domestic violence, perhaps they have not read MacKinnon, but they often subscribe to the premise that men subordinate women through sex and violence.

AB: And what are some of the results of that?

JS: The rise of this powerful theory has been accompanied by the legal embrace of uniformity, mandatory protocols, and the disfavoring of discretion. You have to keep in mind that the overwhelming majority of domestic violence arrests are for misdemeanor crimes, which, by definition, do not involve serious physical injury. Some domestic violence misdemeanors don't even involve physical contact. If the police are called after a man throws an alarm clock on the ground, he may be arrested. The definition of violence itself has expanded to include a lot of conduct that is not physical violence. The working definition of domestic violence today includes conduct like damaging property and stealing from one's spouse, and the harm alleged can be psychological and financial rather than physical. The theory of subordination makes it likely that any man/woman pair who comes into the criminal system will be viewed in these terms. So even for misdemeanors with no physical injury, we tend to think that a woman is being subordinated, and the man who is subordinating her should be punished. In some places, an arrest leads to the issuance of a protection order banning the husband from the family home. Even if the wife says she does not want that, a protection order makes his presence at home a crime for which he can be arrested.

AB: Do you think rape and sexual harassment reflect these changes as well?

JS: Those areas have been part of the same broad process of legal change. We used to think of rape as making a woman have sex by force or threat of force. Just as the definition of violence has expanded beyond physically violent conduct, we now no longer think of coercion in sex as something that necessarily has to happen with the threat of force. In some states, the force element of rape has been eliminated, so that rape is sex without consent. No showing of force or threat of force is required. In the past, coercion might have been viewed as a threat of bodily harm. Today coercion is often understood as a dynamic of unequal power. Simply put, a woman feels she cannot say no. This sense of coercion reflects the belief that power between men and women is almost always unequal, especially in sexual matters. This understanding of sexual subordination also underlies our sexual harassment law. The point is that in many areas that involve relationships between men and women, subordination is now a dominant theory to which our legal system gives effect.

AB: What about family law? Does feminism "govern" in family law?

JS: Family law is an area where we've seen feminist developments that prefer wives over husbands and mothers over fathers. In that process, the legal practices and understandings that we have developed around domestic violence have affected how legal actors view marriage and the family today. What I'm suggesting is that the legal vision of the home has increasingly become that of a man being violent toward his wife. And family law reflects that understanding as well.

AB: How do you mean?

JS: One example would be in divorce. The domestic violence protection orders I mentioned can be obtained without a criminal charge ever being filed. A woman can ask a court to issue an order excluding her husband from the home based on her claim that he has harmed or threatened her, often without the husband having the opportunity to present his side. Of course, in principle, this process could be a good thing if the woman is in danger. But inevitably, some divorce lawyers advise women clients to apply for domestic violence protection orders because it can be used as a powerful tool in the divorce proceeding. Given the expansion of the definition of violence that I mentioned, it really doesn't take that much to show that a threat of violence exists and that a woman needs a protection order. It is not uncommon for domestic violence issues to come into a divorce case in this way. Designed on the assumption of male subordination of women in the home that I've described, the legal system has little means to distinguish orders that actually protect endangered women from those sought for strategic reasons. It is considered dangerous for judges not to issue protection orders when they are requested.

AB: I think masculinity is stigmatized in our courts today. Is it possible that what's happened in the push to reform a sexist legal system that historically treated women unfairly is the rise of a system that now stigmatizes masculinity?

JS: I wouldn't put it that way. But certain behavior like losing one's temper, yelling, throwing things on the ground, or punching an object, say, can now be perceived as sufficient to trigger some extreme results—like being legally banned from your own home and arrested if you return. More men than women find themselves on the wrong side of such situations. And the background for this development is indeed a feminist reform movement that has sought to protect women from violence. Within that paradigm, some things men do in the home when they are frustrated or angry can be put on par with violent acts such as beating their wives or worse. From the idea that husbands who abuse their wives might come to kill them (think O. J. Simpson), it's not a far step to the idea that men whose conduct frightens their wives also might come to do them physical harm. By a chain of association then, it becomes possible to imagine that a man who behaves angrily should be treated like a domestic abuser. It's not that masculinity is stigmatized, but rather that the law is far less tolerant of violence, the definition of domestic and sexual violence has expanded, and a man is viewed as more likely to engage in behavior that falls under that expanded definition. Therefore, the state should do something, like ban his contact with his wife and children.

AB: Do you think that this informs the way courts see divorcing spouses in child custody disputes?

JS: As I mentioned it can be advantageous for the mother to allege conduct that suggests that the father seeking custody might be abusive. In the last fifteen years our courts have come to see domestic violence as a crucial issue in child custody decisions. Many states rightly have a presumption against awarding custody to parents who have engaged in domestic violence. The problem is the relative ease with which legal actors today seem able to view husbands as violent or potentially violent, since the definition of violence has expanded so much. Given that ease, it would be quite surprising if child custody disputes didn't often involve some allegation of violence.

AB: Are fathers disadvantaged in custody disputes in our courts?

JS: Courts used to presume that a young child was better off with the mother. That presumption has largely been abandoned because the legal preference for the mother was based on gender stereotypes. Instead, today a key consideration in custody decisions is who the child's primary caretaker is, and that is a gender-neutral inquiry. Even though courts don't explicitly prefer the mother over the father, the vast majority of primary caretakers are mothers, so the result is not very different from a maternal preference. Fathers who want custody and have not been the primary caretakers of their children have a hard time getting custody.

AB: What do you think of my proposal that there should be a default presumption of joint custody where both parents argue over custody? This presumption could be overcome if one parent is unfit, such as where a father has been abusive?

JS: Parents who want any kind of custody should show that they cared for their children during the marriage. An interesting proposal along those lines is the American Law Institute's proposal, adopted by West Virginia, which aims to allocate custodial responsibility to approximate the time each parent spent caring for the child before the separation. I agree that true abuse should lead to no custody. However, the increasing routineness of violence allegations to claim that a parent is unfit can detract from the effectiveness and fairness of whatever rule one adopts. We need to look more closely at this.

AB: Do you find it surprising that where feminism is in charge, it puts women's interests ahead of men's, the same way that in the past, the legal system put men's interests ahead of women's?

JS: There's no doubt about the violence that feminism sought to address. Perhaps the disadvantages to men are the costs of designing a system that will actually protect women. Surely some women may use the system to serve their interests. Some might say this cost is worth bearing to protect the truly vulnerable. But is it surprising that feminism wields power? No. People have worked hard for feminist legal reform. We're in a tricky phase now where it is essential that we assess the unintended or surprising consequences—for women, men, and children—and ask hard questions about whether this is exactly where we want to be.

15

Admonitions

THE AMERICAN FAMILY law system has degenerated into a disgraceful mess for far too many fathers, mothers, and children. I believe the reason lies in three factors that have developed over the past forty years. The first is the historical conduct of that small group who have abused and/or neglected their wives and families. Every man who abandoned the mother of his child, every man who refused to pay child support or assaulted his wife or beat his children is responsible for the laws we have on the books today. All have contributed. The system we live under today is a response to that behavior, and we must acknowledge that such laws are valid in their intent and purpose.

The second factor is the evolution of family law into an industry. There are judges, lawyers, and therapists who manipulate and take full advantage of the passions, pain, and loss of God-given rights of every man and woman to parent their child. Divorce custody is an increasingly contentious area of family law. More and more men want meaningful custody of their children and want it without the interference of their ex-wives. Those men are willing to fight harder and invest ever-increasing sums of money in order to protect their rights. That is a huge boon to the divorce industry. Any government-funded system is compromised by constraints of budget and time. In the family law system, however, you potentially walk through the looking glass to a place where such constraints do not apply. It is a place where those with little or no money may actually receive a more fair hearing. However, those with greater financial resources are taken for the ride of their lives. Whether you are rich or middle class, famous or keep a low profile, the court will spend your money as if it were their own. Then, they look at you and ask, "You want your child, don't you?" This is one area where the greatest need for change exists. Family law is a racket. It is a racket within which the principal players have convinced even themselves that they are serving innocent children as well as the public. However, the only people they are truly serving are themselves.

As I sat down to write this chapter, I read an article by Jeffrey Toobin, in the February 4, 2008, issue of *The New Yorker* magazine. Toobin, the magazine's legal contributor, details the case of Brian Nichols, who stands accused of multiple murders that took place in an Atlanta courthouse on March 11, 2005. The state of Georgia has spent $1.2 million to provide the capital murder defendant with a reasonable defense. That figure mirrors what I have been forced to spend due to the inefficiencies of the Los Angeles County family law system in order to secure my right to see my daughter. Think about that. Contrast one state, where the defendant in an open-and-shut capital murder case is allocated $1.2 million in legal fees (a move I support, by the way) to another state, where I have to put up that amount to combat parental alienation because judges in Los Angeles do not have the guts to stand up to rapacious lawyers who line their pockets at the expense of men and women victimized by this very real syndrome.

The third factor that has contributed to the problem is the feminist movement. Over time, the feminist movement has leveraged its important and well-deserved courtroom victories regarding domestic violence, rape evidence, and sexual harassment in the workplace into the conditions we now see in American family law. Due to their gains, violence is less tolerated (a good thing), while the definition of what constitutes violent behavior is broadened (a tricky thing). Much of that broadened definition is currently used in divorce litigation to pathologize some of what is perceived as typically male behavior for the purpose of removing men from their homes and keeping them from seeing their kids. (Not always a good thing.)

The accomplishments of the women's rights movement cannot be underestimated. Brave and conscientious women, along with many men, have fought to reemphasize the pain and misery women have endured due to subordination by men and, eventually, to secure women's rights. There are things men typically did to women that are unconscionable and intolerable. Laws were changed to protect the victims. After years of thoughtful discourse and powerful change, family law now provides us with a clear example of where the pendulum has swung too far. The current American criminal and civil law system makes it only too easy for some women to arbitrarily deny many fathers' access to their children.

The right of fathers, not only to see their children, but also to share in a healthy and meaningful level of their custody, is a serious issue in our society. Research has shown that young girls who are raised without fathers are statistically more likely to abuse drugs and alcohol, engage in sexual acts as teenagers and have unsafe sex, and to perform less well in school. I am constantly reminded of the therapist I spoke to who told me that children of both sexes who are alienated from either parent often have marked difficulties in forming attachments to other people and, therefore, lasting and healthy relationships.

Of course, there are men who alienate their children from their mothers. In some ways, this may be even more insidious, as children who are maliciously and wrongly kept from their mothers must suffer in ways that I cannot imagine. However, such cases are far less common. Parental alienation is perpetrated, overwhelmingly, by women against men. It is a violation of those men's rights. Men's rights are subordinated in family law courtrooms in exactly the same way that women's rights had been in the areas of domestic violence, rape, and sexual harassment. Is this what the women's movement intended? A fathers' rights activist told me that, at a hearing at his state legislature to testify for a shared parenting bill, a woman from a group opposing the bill told him, "If a hundred men are accused of spousal abuse and only one is actually guilty, the rest are collateral damage. Even though ninety-nine men lose their rights to see their children, we have saved one woman." If you go to the Web site of the National Organization of Women and read their opposition to the Parental Alienation/DMS inclusion issue, they even insist upon mentioning Richard Gardner's suicide, as if Gardner's decision to end his own life in any way negates his work studying children.

IF YOU ARE CONTEMPLATING DIVORCE, you will likely need all the help you can get. Here are some suggestions I offer regarding divorce decision-making. There is also a need for change in our family law procedures. I therefore make certain recommendations, each of which has grown out of my seven years of experience within this system.

1. GET A PRENUP

Even though some important issues litigated in family law cannot be covered by a prenuptial agreement, such as most custody arrangements, a prenup gives the court a snapshot of each party's thinking at the time of the marriage. I would go so far as to say that states should offer prospective spouses prenuptial counseling. Even if this comes down to a simple pamphlet, people should be given information at the very time of the blood test and licensing that explains how a prenup can save them time, money, and some degree of pain should they choose to dissolve their marriage. The law cannot compel someone to enter into such an agreement, but it can shed light on that option. As I have said countless times to people when the subject comes up, get a prenup so you have a document that has been executed while you still have a shred of respect for each other.

2. FILE FIRST

Many people are often too confused or torn to file for divorce. However, filing first has distinct advantages. To be the plaintiff in such proceedings is to be the one making the

complaint. To a degree, you frame the debate. You set the
tone. To be the defendant in a divorce proceeding leaves you
counter-punching much of the time. Many people, particularly men, told me that they wanted to do the "kinder" thing
by allowing their wife to file. Or they did not want their
children to believe that they had filed first. This can create
real problems. If you believe in your heart that it's over, file.
You can always rescind later.

3. DO NOT HIRE YOUR LAWYER BASED ON
WORD OF MOUTH

Every divorce is different. Just because some tough lawyer
got results for your friend does not mean that this is the
right lawyer for you. You will have to work with this person
on what may be one of the most difficult tasks of your life.
You want someone you can relate to, in some fashion. You
must work hard and quickly and interview several different
lawyers. Choose one who is not only skilled but also is someone you can talk to. In my own case, Bob Kaufman was a
good lawyer. Dennis Wasser was a good lawyer. But I just
couldn't stand being in the room with either of them for any
length of time. Vicki Greene, the attorney I have used for
most of my case, has had her wins and losses. She has han-
dled some things in ways that have caused me real concern.
Overall, however, I am grateful for having met her and for
having her serve as my attorney.

4. HAVE YOUR ATTORNEY EXPLAIN IN DETAIL
WHAT LIES AHEAD

Even though things may not follow the scenario they paint
for you, you want your attorney to lay out what the beats of

the case will likely be. You want your attorney to tell you what outside experts will need to be hired and at what cost. You also want your attorney to tell you their strategy for settling the case.

5. MEDIATE ONLY IF YOUR SPOUSE IS MEDIATION MATERIAL

Remember Jane Shatz's remark: all behavior is consistent. If your ex has shown themselves capable of the type of dialogue and compromise mediation requires, if you firmly believe that your ex genuinely seeks a mediated settlement, then mediate. Otherwise, go to court. Court is a tremendous compromise for any rational human being, but you will lose precious time with your child if you gamble on a program of ultimately bogus mediation, only to have that collapse and end up in front of a judge anyway.

6. CONSTRUCT A TIME LINE FOR YOUR MEDIATION

Mediation does you little good if it drags on. For example, if there are no established grounds to deny you custody, you should have interim custody orders in place within ninety days of separation. If your entire mediation lasts more than six months, consider going to court. Some lawyers use the bait of mediation to kill time. Then they hit the eject button and you end up in court anyway, having spent under a hundred hours with your child in the past six months. Insist that there be a timetable to resolve each area of negotiation. Most important, insist that custody issues be addressed immediately. Unless there are reasons why your custody should be interrupted, you want a schedule to see your children to be established right away, even if it serves only as an interim schedule.

7. DEMAND IN MEDIATION (OR PETITION FOR IN COURT) THAT YOU AND YOUR EX ATTEND A *MINIMUM* OF TWELVE SESSIONS OF DIVORCE CO–PARENTING COUNSELING IF YOU BELIEVE THAT ALIENATION IS A FACTOR IN YOUR CASE

The attending therapist should have the responsibility of reporting to the judge on the progress of the two litigants and should have the right to recommend additional sessions if they believe they are required. Parental alienation often grows over time. Children adjust to and compensate for the alienating pressures in their lives. Addressing these negative forces that act upon your child, and doing so early on, is crucial. Make this among your top priorities.

8. DO NOT HIDE ASSETS

If in your financial settlement you hide your assets, you will get slammed. Pay your support and pay it on time. Failure to meet your support obligations is among the easiest ways to negatively impact your case for custody.

9. SET UP A FEW SESSIONS WITH A THERAPIST WHO WORKS IN FAMILY LAW

Do this prior to entering into the custody phase of your case. I went into the custody evaluation phase of my case blind. I did not know what criteria custody evaluators use as the basis for their recommendations to the court. That is why I recommend to individuals that they schedule an appointment with a family therapist, particularly one who serves as a court-appointed custody evaluator, prior to your first meeting with the evaluator assigned to your case. Do not ask them to coach you. You simply want them to explain the process. Ask them what evaluators look for in such evaluative sessions. *Do not* rely on your attorneys to help you.

10. FIND YOUR JANE SHATZ

Find that therapist you can trust who will guide you through the changes and decisions that you will certainly encounter. You will want a second opinion about when you should bend and when to hold fast regarding the way you parent your child after divorce. How do you maintain your child's respect for you as a noncustodial parent? You should seek advice about how to introduce your child to your new home, your new life, and the new people in it.

11. DO NOT MAKE YOUR HOME A SHRINE TO YOUR CHILD

I made this mistake myself until a doctor told me that to live in such a suspended state was unhealthy. Enveloping yourself in memories or surrounding yourself with photos of your child, for example, will only prolong the pain and stunt your own growth. Your child will grow and move on with their life, and you must do the same. It is how you choose to do these things that matters most.

12. PUT YOUR AND/OR YOUR EX'S DRUG AND ALCOHOL ISSUES ON THE TABLE

You can bet that the lawyers on the other side will potentially bury you over allegations of drug or alcohol abuse, so do not hesitate to raise such issues on the part of your ex.

Similarly, come clean with your lawyer regarding your own patterns of behavior. I met a man who believed his casual marijuana habit was "no big deal." However, this issue was raised during his trial, and as a result he lost all custody of his kids. His ex left town and relocated to another city. Now he flies a very long distance to see his children very infrequently.

13. ASK FOR ORDERS, IN COURT OR IN MEDIATION, THAT PROVIDE FOR SOME FLEXIBILITY OF SCHEDULE, PARTICULARLY IN TERMS OF YOUR WORK AND CAREER

Do not hesitate to ask that you have the right to change your schedule for a limited and specified number of times per year. You have the right to work and to be reliable in your profession. That reliability may require that you amend your visitation/custody schedule. Make sure your attorney addresses that during your proceedings. Also, ask for right of first refusal!

In addition to these steps, which can help you take control of your own divorce, I believe the family law system itself needs to be reformed, especially as it impacts custody decisions. Therefore, I believe the following areas of family law need to be addressed:

1. The *very moment* that one parent is out of the house as the result of separation papers being filed (let alone divorce papers), both of those individuals should be ordered by a judge to go to divorced co-parenting sessions. If you are divorcing and you and your spouse are able to reach a viable

custody arrangement, then you may not need divorce co-parenting therapy. However, wherever the potential for parental alienation exists, then it must be headed off and early. *Do not wait* until the phones are disconnected and your ex files some bogus order of protection. This is one of the greatest disgraces of the family law system in this country. Parental alienation thrives when one parent has the benefit of contiguous periods of time to influence his or her child. Often that time is gained by the gamesmanship of destructive lawyers. An immediate court order for an indeterminate number of such sessions has the potential to do more to counter the overwhelming force of PAS than any other legal or therapeutic reform. Once assigned, that therapist should be obligated to report to the judge on the progress of the participants.

2. Laws need to be amended regarding custody evaluation and evaluators. Evaluations need to be speeded up and conducted on very specific timetables. Litigants, both male and female, deserve to receive timely long-term custody orders, and to the extent that evaluations play a role in determining those orders, they should be conducted as expeditiously as possible. Evaluators should be assigned, blind, by judges from a pool of therapists. Your lawyer is not always the best judge of what evaluator will give you the fairest treatment. Not by a long shot. Lawyers and judges should not have much discretion in these assignments at all. Evaluators pass judgment on litigants much as juries do, therefore, they should be subject to a limited number of preemptive challenges, just as jurors are.

3. I believe that the default position of any court should be fifty-fifty custody. Unless there are compelling reasons,

backed by evidence, that either parent is unfit and should, thus, have their custody reduced or withheld, either parent should qualify for one-half. Period. I believe God gave people two parents for a reason, not just so one could get a job, pay the bills, and rarely see their kids. In practical terms, however, we are still far from that reality. In West Virginia, courts want "to allocate custodial responsibility so that the proportion of custodial time the child spends with each parent approximates the proportion of time each parent spent performing caretaking functions for the child prior to the parents' separation."[1] Assuming that you were a conscientious and available dad during your marriage, under this law you would be eligible for that same opportunity as a divorced dad. That seems fair.

IN 2006, Justice Judith Kaye, chief judge of New York, oversaw the Miller Commission, designed to examine reforms in New York's divorce law. Named for New York Supreme Court justice Sondra Miller, the Miller Commission's report pressed for the passage of no-fault divorce laws in New York and for more mediation of cases, outside of the courts, in pursuit of "collaborative divorce" proceedings. In an interview contained in *Judicial Reports*, Miller is quoted as saying, "Mediation is a far more humane and better process for resolving these disputes, rather than litigation."[2] A New York

---

[1] *West's Annotated Code of West Virginia Currentness*, chapter 48: Domestic Relations, article 9: Custody of Children, part 2: Parenting Plan, section 48-9-206: Allocation of custodial responsibility.

[2] "Exclusive Interviews: Ex-Judge Pushes Divorce Reforms," www.judicialreports.com/2007/04/exclusive_interview_exjudge_pu.php (accessed May 19, 2008).

Supreme Court justice believes that you would be better off staying out of court. Based on my experiences in Los Angeles, I would have to agree.

I call it "successful divorce." Some reform advocates call it collaborative divorce. Either way, our society has an urgent need for reform in the area of family law. A staggering number of men and women are impacted by the madness of divorce and custody law as it is adjudicated in American courts. Countless others are impacted, secondarily, by the effects that these injustices have on someone they love. Most significantly affected are the children of divorce: the millions of Americans who grow up suffering as the result of divorce battles and thus carry the scars with them into adult life. Much of this painful reality is unnecessary and could be eliminated by simply casting some light onto what really happens within this country's system. Where there are children involved, successful divorce means an agreement that has the least negative effect on the children. If someone is abusive or neglectful, that is determinative. Similarly, parental alienation is child abuse and it should be determinative of child custody in equal measure to any other factor considered.

I REMEMBER VISITING a college class where the discussion of the evolution of women's rights in the courts followed the same course as it had at Harvard. With all of the talk of rape evidence, sexual harassment, and the violent abuse of women by men, I saw one young student crying quietly in her seat. When the class was over, I approached her and asked her what it was that had triggered her response. She said, "My mom and dad fought over my custody.

I had to drive a long distance between each of their homes every other week. It affected every part of my childhood. It was horrible." The tears streamed down the girl's face. In her eyes, it seemed as if the tragedy of her parents' unsuccessful divorce was there, all these years later, in the classroom with her, once again.

Afterword

IF YOU THINK I wrote this book in order to settle a score, you are wrong. As I stated in the introduction, I never wanted to write this book. Almost two years have passed since I first began working on it, and nothing has changed. In fact, my desire to turn my attention away from this subject has only grown stronger. Any animosity I might have had has been processed and, thankfully, is gone by now. I did not write this book to attack or denigrate certain people or individual members of any profession. I am well aware of the fact that the average person who operates inside the divorce system could never be expected to stand up to it. Lawyers and judges and court-appointed therapists have been left, for decades, to make their own rules inside a closed environment. Actually, I am somewhat surprised that there is not even more abuse than exists already.

In fact, I blame my ex-wife least of all for what has transpired. She is a person, like many of us, doing the best she can with what she has. She is a litigant and, therefore, one who walks into a courtroom and is never offered anything other than what is served there. Nothing off the menu, ever. Conflict escalation is what happens in too many family law courtrooms. In California, it is an epidemic. The people who are to blame are the lawyers, the therapists, the legislators, and, most insidiously of all, the judges. They are the cogs in a closed system, one that they have allowed to evolve principally for their own enrichment, financial or otherwise.

There is much that I left out of this book. There are stories, facts, and opinions that have been omitted, some of it detrimental even to me, because court records have been sealed. Some, however, were omitted because I have no desire to accomplish anything other than to draw attention to the issue of parental alienation. I certainly do not need to stir the pot any further regarding my own case. If some of those who stand in the way of exposing that issue get rattled, so be it. It is important that I state that no one I criticize in these pages has broken any laws. No one has done anything that proved to be actionable in any civil court. No attorneys, judges, or court-appointed therapists were held in contempt of court, nor were any of them found to be in violation of any code of professional ethics. Perhaps, that is part of the problem. The issue is one of fairness and competence. Incompetent men and women, operating in the family law system, are rendering judgments against fathers that are biased and violate their rights as parents. Many judges are overwhelmed by the politics of custody. In giving more time to one parent, the time of the other parent is necessarily reduced. If a parent who suffers such a net reduction should be a woman, somehow that is seen as a setback for women's rights. Sometimes it seems that a call to acknowledge the validity of fatherhood itself is viewed, by some politically driven groups, as an affront to women's rights.

In my father's day, men worked and women kept the house and little was debated about that. Today, many fathers, divorced or not, want a significant role in raising their children. They make important decisions around their child care responsibilities. Saturdays that used to mean a round of golf are now often spent at a child's soccer game or ballet recital. I know men who are captains of industry who consistently sacrifice their own free time and happily place their kids among their highest priorities. For many men, fathering has become a part of their public identity. If both the mother and father are professionals, wherein is it written that the mother's nanny or sister or mother is better able to care for the child simply because that person represents a decision the mother has made? There are, however, many cases where that kind of thinking still prevails.

Men have fewer rights in a family law courtroom than women do. There is the tired presumption that men are less interested in parenting their children on a meaningful level. It is also presumed that they are less capable. There are too many good men, and some women, who have had or are currently having their parental rights improperly taken away from them. How is any of this in a child's best interest? How much of what we currently tolerate inside a family law courtroom is the result of institutional greed, bad legislation, corruption, and politics?

If you think that this is a men's issue, you are wrong. Some of the greatest proponents of bringing the problem of parental alienation into the light are women. Typically, that woman is someone who currently loves a man who is the victim of PAS. She knows what a good father he is. She sees how the alienating ex arbitrarily and maliciously interferes with or outright destroys his relationship with his children. As the man struggles, his new wife or girlfriend struggles alongside him. She shares in a large part of his suffering. She wishes there were something she could do to alter the situation. Some of the angriest voices I have encountered attacking the sickness of PAS have come from women who have watched a target parent undeservedly suffer.

I have also spoken with second wives who have witnessed the miracle of constructive co-parenting for their husband and his ex after an abysmal divorce. One woman told me of how she and her husband battled his ex for custody for several years. The mutual hatred was palpable and ever present. Today, she informed me, they are all elements of a loving family. "She is the godmother of my daughter," she told me. "My child with her ex-husband. Can you imagine?" Actually, I can. It is human nature to overcome adversity and to move beyond unhealthy emotional unrest and resentments. But what if you want to foster constructive co-parenting and your ex does not? What can you do? If a marriage is unsuccessful, the principals must be encouraged to move on. They must be encouraged and facilitated toward that end by friends, family, and especially the courts.

Some of the other angry voices I heard were those of mothers and sisters who watched their son or brother suffer, wishing they could help. Their loved one is on the painful end of a bad divorce. They know that man, often better than his exwife does. They watch him suffer and wish there was something they could do to help. Colleagues, friends, in-laws, and kindred spirits all wonder how any woman (all of whom have fathers and who either have or wished for a better relationship with their own dad) could put someone through this.

Inarguably, there are women who are victims of PAS themselves. Usually through drug charges, a history of alcohol abuse, or an arrest record of some kind, men go into court, aided and abetted by a male-leaning judge and/or evaluator, and take children away from their mothers. The effect is the same. Children need two parents, where two parents exist, ready, willing, and able to carry out their role.

If you think there is nothing you can do about this problem, you are wrong. There are many well-organized groups of passionate and reasonable men who are taking the cause of parental alienation to the courts and legislatures. These groups have formerly been called fathers' rights groups, but in an attempt to remove the gender-specific exclusion of that phrase, they are now often referred to as parents' rights groups. On the Internet, their presence is significant. Some fathers' rights organizations, unfortunately, have an unconcealed misogyny surrounding their agenda. They attack some perpetrators of PAS as much for being women as for anything else. That course, however, is both unjust and futile. Parents' rights groups must reach out to both men and women, just as the women's movement has done, if they are to gain any ground. Contact your state legislator to find out what bills your state is considering in order to reform divorce and family law where you reside. Visit a parents' rights Web site to see what developments regarding family law reform are evolving, like those in West Virginia, or those proposed by the Miller Commission in New York.

Most important, don't give up on your child. My own battle

in court was the worst thing I have ever dealt with: worse than the death of my dad, worse than the end of any relationship (including my marriage), worse than any career reversal I have ever experienced. I wanted to give up many times. I know there are countless others who now feel or have felt the same. However, a therapist whom I met with in New York emphasized to me the concept of latent learning. Everything you say, everything you do that is communicated to your child, is recorded, both in the child's mind and soul. He told me that one day, regardless of my skepticism, everything I have done will be remembered. Every joke I told, every trip we took, every odd or silly moment. Every instruction I gave or mistake I made; all the good and all the bad. Your child may not bring it up. But it is in there. You are a part of your child. You are half of your child. Do not ever, ever forget that. No matter how hard it gets.

It is those promises that we make to ourselves that can cause us the greatest pain. When I married my wife, I promised myself that I would cherish that relationship until death did us part. I broke that promise. When I divorced, I promised myself that I would not allow my divorce to become my daughter's problem. I broke that promise. I promised myself I would never give up on my daughter and, for a brief period last year, I broke that promise, as well. In April of 2006, I promised myself that I would write this book, to help people better understand the terrible and unnecessary pain that the divorce industry inflicts on those people who have the bad fortune to enter their world.

Working on this book these past two years has been like fixing a car while driving it. At different points, I just kept adding new chapters, depending on what development my case threw at me. I wish I had more time to do more research, to interview more lawyers and legal scholars, more victims and their families, and more children of divorce. I wish I were a better writer and had found a way to more effectively communicate what this experience has meant to me. In the end, I wish that there was no need for a book on this subject at all. But I fulfilled this promise. I love my daughter with all my heart. And, with all my heart, I hope that this book benefits other men, and women, who love their children. I hope it helps others to fulfill the promises they have made to their families and themselves.

Acknowledgments

I WOULD LIKE TO thank my literary agent, Karen Gantz Zahler, for her unflagging support and encouragement during the composition of this book. Also, the administration and staff of St. Martin's Press, for publishing the book and for their invaluable guidance throughout. In particular I would like to thank Sally Richardson, Charles Spicer, Jennifer Enderlin, Yaniv Soha, Frances Sayers, John Murphy, Steve Troha, Courtney Fischer, and Steve Snider.

My thanks to Dr. Jane Shatz, Dr. Ray DiGiuseppe, Dr. Mike Flaxmann, Dr. Christina Lindstrom, Sheila Reisel, and Harvard professor Jeannie Suk, for their contributions to my understanding of the legal and therapeutic analysis of family law.

Love and thanks to my brothers and sisters, Beth, Daniel, Billy, Jane, and Stephen; to Jessica Ambrose, David Black, Ron Dobson, Herb Berman, and Jeff Colle; and to my nieces, nephews, and friends, all who endured my whining these many years.

Particular thanks to Vicki Greene, who saw and heard it all.

My thanks to Hannah Tabb, unflappable transcription artiste extraordinaire.

And to Mark Tabb, a partner and good friend throughout.